AF614894

PILGRIM OF PRAYER

JOURNAL

In case of loss, please return to:

TABLE OF CONTENTS

In the inner stillness
where meditation leads,
the Spirit secretly anoints
the soul and heals our
deepest wounds.

St. John of the Cross

WELCOME

Dear Pilgrim,

Welcome to the Pilgrim of Prayer Journal, a daily companion crafted to deepen your connection with God and draw you into a richer, more fulfilling prayer life. Inspired by the prayer habits of Christian mystics, this journal is designed to help you walk the sacred path of Christian meditation, one of the Church's most profound spiritual practices.

As you begin this journey, remember that you are not alone. You are joining a community of fellow pilgrims within the Saintmaker family who seek to know, love, and serve God in all things. Together, we are striving to live with greater wisdom, peace, and reliance on His divine will. Whether you're just beginning or have been on this path for some time, this journal will guide you, strengthen you, and encourage you.

May this journey transform your prayer life, helping you find deeper communion with the Lord each day. We are honored to be part of your spiritual pilgrimage, and we look forward to walking this sacred journey alongside you.

Welcome to Pilgrim of Prayer and the Saintmaker community!

HOW TO USE THIS JOURNAL

The Pilgrim of Prayer Journal is designed to help you cultivate a daily prayer life rooted in the rich tradition of Christian mystics. Whether you're new to mental prayer and contemplation or looking to deepen your practice, this journal will guide you through daily meditations, reflections, and your Evening Examen. The structure is simple yet profound, offering you the space to listen, reflect, and respond to God's movements in your soul.

To make the most of this journal, we encourage you to develop a consistent routine. Each day presents an opportunity to go deeper into your spiritual life, offering prompts for reflection and prayer. While there are no strict rules, following these steps will help you get the most out of each session and draw closer to God.

Here's a general overview of how to use the daily pages:

COMPLETE YOUR MORNING SESSION

- ***Set aside a dedicated time and place for meditation each morning.*** This will help you create a routine and make it easier to enter into a prayerful mindset.
- ***Choose a resource for your meditation.*** This could be a spiritual book, a Scripture passage, or another resource you find spiritually enriching (see page 11 for suggestions).
- ***Follow the prompts in the journal*** to complete your meditation, taking time to observe, reflect, converse with God, and consider how to act on your insights.
- ***Spend a few extra moments in gratitude***, thanking God for His presence and guidance in your life.

COMPLETE YOUR JOURNAL ENTRY AND EVENING EXAMEN

During the day, jot down any spiritual notes in the "Journal Entry" section. These could be lessons learned, blessings received, or difficulties you've encountered.

At the end of the day, review those notes or use the space to reflect on your day as a whole. End your day with the Evening Examen, following the time-honored tradition of St. Ignatius of Loyola. The Examen will guide you to reflect on where God was present throughout your day and will offer insight and peace as you prepare for tomorrow.

OPTIONAL: USE THE STREAK TRACKER

The Streak Tracker can help you stay motivated and accountable by marking your daily prayer streaks. Record your progress and challenge yourself to build longer and more consistent prayer habits over time.

If you're already using The Saintmaker Catholic Life Planner, Pilgrim of Prayer can serve as an ideal companion. The journal enhances the "Meditation Journal" section of the Saintmaker by providing additional structure for deeper reflection. Use Pilgrim of Prayer to guide your morning meditation, and then record the results of your Evening Examen in your Saintmaker planner for a well-rounded spiritual experience.

We encourage you to take your time with each step, knowing that prayer is a journey. The Pilgrim of Prayer Journal is designed to help you stay on the path, giving you the tools and inspiration to deepen your relationship with God each day.

ON CHRISTIAN MEDITATION

Christian meditation, also known as mental or contemplative prayer, is a transformational practice that can radically deepen your understanding of the Faith and your relationship with God. It opens a new window to see how God is working in your life day by day. Through meditation, what once appeared ordinary can be illuminated with spiritual clarity, helping you recognize God's will in situations and empowering you to rely on His guidance more fully.

If you embark on this path, you will soon notice how the practice brings peace into your daily life. The distractions and stresses of the world begin to lose their hold as you become more centered on Christ. With time and patience, meditation helps the soul to focus, calming the mind and recollecting the heart in ways that affect both prayer life and everyday actions. This sense of peace and recollection becomes a lasting gift, one that continues to grow as the practice deepens.

But the journey of meditation is not without its challenges. One of the most common obstacles is the tendency for prayer to become repetitive or mechanical. Often, we rely on set prayers. These prayers, while beneficial, can leave us stuck in routine. St. Teresa of Ávila, a master of contemplation, emphasized that true prayer is not about the words we say but about the personal encounter with God. Meditation invites us to go beyond repetition, to make our prayer personal, alive, and sincere. As St. Francis de Sales advised, we are called to "breathe life" into our prayer by entering into it with our whole heart and soul.

For many, mental prayer is the doorway to discovering that prayer is not separate from daily life but rather its animating feature. This is a lesson taught by the saints and confirmed in the experience of those who practice meditation. In St. John of the Cross's teachings, we learn that prayer aligns us with God's will, conforming us to His divine plan and making us receptive to His grace. As our prayer life deepens, we begin to understand that everything we do—whether it's working, interacting with others, or engaging in small, mundane tasks—can be a prayer offered to God. Through meditation, we cultivate the habit of living in God's presence.

The key to consistency in this journey lies in creating a sacred space for prayer. Having a dedicated place in your home where you can meet God in the quiet of early morning, before the world stirs to life, can help establish a meaningful routine. As St. Francis de Sales once advised, "Half an hour's meditation each day is essential, except when you are busy. Then a full hour is needed." Establishing a consistent time for prayer not only frames the day with a spiritual focus but also helps ensure that we don't neglect this vital practice.

In addition to a sacred space, it's helpful to revisit the fruits of your meditation throughout the day. St. Teresa often emphasized the importance of recalling the graces received in prayer, allowing them to nourish your soul during moments of distraction or difficulty. Writing down insights and reviewing them later can keep the connection to your prayer life alive and active as the day progresses. By the time you reach the Evening Examen, you'll be able to see more clearly how God's grace has influenced your actions, decisions, and thoughts throughout the day.

As St. John of the Cross taught, meditation is less about seeking answers and more about waiting for God to gradually unveil Himself to the soul. There will be times of spiritual dryness when the mind feels distracted or it seems as though God is silent. These moments are not signs of failure but invitations to deeper trust and patience. God often works most powerfully in the quiet, hidden recesses of the soul, even when we cannot perceive it. The key is to remain faithful to the practice, trusting that He is working in ways beyond our understanding.

One powerful tool for perseverance during these times is the use of visualization, a practice that can help reignite spiritual focus. St. Teresa of Ávila often encouraged her nuns to visualize scenes from Scripture, such as Christ in the garden or at the Cross. Through this method, the soul can enter more fully into prayer, allowing God to speak not just to the intellect but to the heart. With time, this practice becomes a natural way to immerse oneself in the mysteries of God's love and guidance.

As you progress in your journey of meditation, remember that this is not a race but a lifelong pilgrimage. St. Francis de Sales reminded us that "nothing is so strong as gentleness, nothing so gentle as real strength." Approach each day with humility, knowing that prayer is a gift to be received, not an accomplishment to be checked off a list. It's through this humble and open attitude that we grow in intimacy with God, allowing Him to shape our hearts and our lives in ways we may not immediately see but will ultimately transform us.

The journey of Christian meditation is one of discovery. It deepens our spiritual awareness and opens us to God's will. While it can be challenging at times, it leads to profound peace and intimacy with the Lord. The saints remind us that perseverance, patience, and openness are key to deepening our prayer lives. Trust in the process, rely on God's grace, and know that He is guiding you every step of the way.

Contemplation is not just about thinking; it is about experiencing God's presence in our lives and letting that experience guide us in every action.

St. Francis de Sales

TIPS AND TRICKS

When you encounter spiritual dryness or hit a rough spot in your prayer life, remember these tips:

- ***Set a regular time for meditation*** – Consistency builds habit. Stick to a schedule even when it feels difficult.
- ***Keep it simple*** – On difficult days, shorten your prayer time but keep the appointment.
- ***Turn to Scripture*** – Let the Word of God guide your meditation and provide new insights.
- ***Use spiritual reading*** – Books by saints or spiritual authors can reignite your passion for prayer.
- ***Be patient with yourself*** – Dryness is part of the journey; don't get discouraged by slow progress.
- ***Pray for perseverance*** – Ask God for the grace to keep going when it feels challenging.
- ***Review past journal entries*** – Reflect on previous spiritual insights to reignite your devotion.
- ***Stay humble*** – Trust that even in silence, God is working in your soul.

SPIRITUAL READING FOR MEDITATION

- Psalms
- The four Gospels
- *Divine Intimacy*
Father Gabriel of St. Mary Magdalen, O.C.D
- *Imitation of Christ*
Thomas à Kempis
- *Preparation for Death*
St. Alphonsus Liguori
- *The Spiritual Combat*
Lorenzo Scupoli

SAMPLE PAGES

Step 1: Read a scriptural quote to place yourself into God's presence. →

Step 2: Summarize the subject of your meditation here. →

Step 3: Spend 5+ minutes in meditation on the subject →

Step 4: Take note of what stood out for you in your meditation. →

Step 5: Reflect on the meaning of these observations for your life. →

Step 6: Talk with God about what He wants you to learn from this session →

Step 7: Choose an action to make your meditation practical. →

Session 3 | 6/15/25 | Source: Imitation of Christ, III:19 | Adoration: (Y) / N

GOD'S PRESENCE

"Be still, and know that I am God! I am exalted among the nations, I am exalted in the earth." – **Psalm 46:10**

Subject *Write or describe the **quotation, scene or event,** or **mystery** that you will meditate on.*

"He is not truly a patient man who will suffer no more than he thinks good and from whom it pleases him ... What thou sufferest is but little in comparison to those who have suffered so much."

✓ SPIRITUAL QUOTATION | ○ SCENE OR EVENT | ○ MYSTERY OF FAITH

MEDITATION

– **Spiritual quotation:** Read and reread the quotation deliberately and meditatively.

– **Scene or Event:** Attempt to place yourself into the scene as a participant or as an observer.

– **Mystery of Faith:** Make comparisons and analogies ("the Kingdom of Heaven is like ...").

Observe *What main ideas or impressions stood out during meditation?*

1. It is easy to be good when you avoid trials.
2. What most of us suffer is little compared with the saints or our Lord.
3. We try to decide what type of suffering is "good" or "enough," but that's not our job.

Reflect *What seems significant about these observations for your life right now?*

1. I try to avoid trials by "having the perfect plan," or being clever.
2. True! The past few months have been tough, but God is being merciful.
3. I experience anger, frustration, and despair when I don't accept suffering that God allows.

Converse *How is God speaking to your heart through this meditation?*

"I love you and I will never let you fall. You do not always understand what it is that I am doing for you, but you don't need to. You need to have faith. I want you to attend Mass more often. Please try to go to Mass at least one more time during the week. This will help you accept My will."

Act *What practical step can you take to bring your meditation to life in your actions today?*

Go to bed early so I can go to Mass tomorrow + pray my Rosary.

20 PILGRIM OF PRAYER JOURNAL

JOURNAL ENTRY

"Let the words of my mouth and the meditation of my heart be acceptable in your sight, O Lord, my rock and my redeemer."

PSALM 19:14

+ When I spoke with Jen this morning and I did a good job (by God's grace) to not get caught up in it, but instead provide some valuable supportive words and perspective.

- Annoyed at how spread out other people are on other projects. Need to revisit the commitments we all made at our project meeting and to ask if anything needs to change. I am attached to a certain outcome, and I need to take time to see it more clearly by slowing down and listening.

+ I prayed the "Come Holy Spirit" prayer before my meeting. It brought me peace and confidence, and I was amazed at how present everyone seemed to be and how carefully they all listened to each other. Thanks be to God!

- Need to rely more on God. If I am not open to His blessings through prayer, then how can I expect Him to support me or how can I be sure that I'll even recognize His blessings when they come?

• Remember tomorrow: bring a sense of peace to my work, ask for God's help, rely on Him, and be honest with James about what I think is needed for the project.

+ Took time to play with Peter after work, and it was the highlight of my day! He loves exploring the woods and fields behind our house, and he eats and sleeps better when we do.

EVENING EXAMEN

Examine your conscience about the thoughts, words, deeds, and omissions of this day. Then, with true repentance, pray an **Act of Contrition**: "O my God, I am heartily sorry for having offended Thee, and I detest all my sins because of Thy just punishments, but most of all because they offend Thee, my God, who art all good and deserving of all my love. I firmly resolve with the help of Thy grace to sin no more and to avoid the near occasion of sin. Amen."

Our Father. Hail Mary. Glory Be.

PILGRIM OF PRAYER JOURNAL 21

← **Journal:** Keep track of spiritual insights throughout the day.

Optional: Code journal entries as follows:

+ Positive
- Challenge
• Neutral

This will help you in your Evening Examen!

← **Examen:** At the end of your day, perform an Evening Examen. Review your journal entries for spiritual victories, struggles, and more, or reflect on the day in the space provided.

MONTH 1

THE FOUNDATIONS OF PRAYER

As you start your three-month journey, this month focuses on preparing for a consistent daily meditation practice. Take time to reflect on how you can create an environment that supports your spiritual growth and sets you up for success.

What time and place will you set for daily meditation to create peace and focus?

What goals do you have for your relationship with God through this journey?

How will you stay committed to meditation, even on difficult days?

What Scriptures or readings will guide your daily practice?

How will you trust God's work, even when progress feels slow?

Session 1 | / / | Source: | Adoration? Y / N

GOD'S PRESENCE

"Do not fear, for I am with you, do not be afraid, for I am your God; I will strengthen you, I will help you ..." – **Isaiah 41:10**

Subject *Write or describe the* ***quotation, scene or event,*** *or* ***mystery*** *that you will meditate on.*

○ SPIRITUAL QUOTATION | ○ SCENE OR EVENT | ○ MYSTERY OF FAITH

MEDITATION

→ **Spiritual quotation:** Read and reread the quotation deliberately and meditatively.

→ **Scene or Event:** Attempt to place yourself into the scene as a participant or as an observer.

→ **Mystery of Faith:** Make comparisons and analogies ("the Kingdom of Heaven is like ...").

Observe *What main ideas or impressions stood out during meditation?*

Reflect *What seems significant about these observations for your life right now?*

Converse *How is God speaking to your heart through this meditation?*

Act *What practical step can you take to bring your meditation to life in your actions today?*

JOURNAL ENTRY

"But when you pray, go into your room and shut the door and pray to your Father who is in secret; your Father who sees in secret will reward you."

MATTHEW 6:6

EVENING EXAMEN

Examine your conscience about the thoughts, words, deeds, and omissions of this day. Then, with true repentance, pray an **Act of Contrition**: "O my God, I am heartily sorry for having offended Thee, and I detest all my sins because of Thy just punishments, but most of all because they offend Thee, my God, who art all good and deserving of all my love. I firmly resolve with the help of Thy grace to sin no more and to avoid the near occasion of sin. Amen."

Our Father. Hail Mary. Glory Be.

Session 2 | / / | Source: | Adoration? Y / N

GOD'S PRESENCE

"... Be strong and courageous; do not be frightened or dismayed, for the Lord your God is with you ..." – **Joshua 1:9**

Subject *Write or describe the **quotation, scene or event,** or **mystery** that you will meditate on.*

○ SPIRITUAL QUOTATION | ○ SCENE OR EVENT | ○ MYSTERY OF FAITH

MEDITATION

→ **Spiritual quotation:** Read and reread the quotation deliberately and meditatively.

→ **Scene or Event:** Attempt to place yourself into the scene as a participant or as an observer.

→ **Mystery of Faith:** Make comparisons and analogies ("the Kingdom of Heaven is like ...").

Observe *What main ideas or impressions stood out during meditation?*

Reflect *What seems significant about these observations for your life right now?*

Converse *How is God speaking to your heart through this meditation?*

Act *What practical step can you take to bring your meditation to life in your actions today?*

JOURNAL ENTRY

"The Spirit helps us in our weakness; we do not know how to pray as we ought, but the Spirit himself intercedes for us with sighs too deep for words."

ROMANS 8:26

EVENING EXAMEN

Examine your conscience about the thoughts, words, deeds, and omissions of this day. Then, with true repentance, pray an **Act of Contrition**: "O my God, I am heartily sorry for having offended Thee, and I detest all my sins because of Thy just punishments, but most of all because they offend Thee, my God, who art all good and deserving of all my love. I firmly resolve with the help of Thy grace to sin no more and to avoid the near occasion of sin. Amen."

Our Father. Hail Mary. Glory Be.

Session 3 | / / | Source: | Adoration? Y / N

GOD'S PRESENCE

"Be still, and know that I am God! I am exalted among the nations, I am exalted in the earth." – **Psalm 46:10**

Subject *Write or describe the **quotation, scene or event,** or **mystery** that you will meditate on.*

○ SPIRITUAL QUOTATION | ○ SCENE OR EVENT | ○ MYSTERY OF FAITH

MEDITATION

→ **Spiritual quotation:** Read and reread the quotation deliberately and meditatively.

→ **Scene or Event:** Attempt to place yourself into the scene as a participant or as an observer.

→ **Mystery of Faith:** Make comparisons and analogies ("the Kingdom of Heaven is like ...").

Observe *What main ideas or impressions stood out during meditation?*

Reflect *What seems significant about these observations for your life right now?*

Converse *How is God speaking to your heart through this meditation?*

Act *What practical step can you take to bring your meditation to life in your actions today?*

JOURNAL ENTRY

"Let the words of my mouth and the meditation of my heart be acceptable in your sight, O Lord, my rock and my redeemer."

PSALM 19:14

EVENING EXAMEN

Examine your conscience about the thoughts, words, deeds, and omissions of this day. Then, with true repentance, pray an **Act of Contrition**: "O my God, I am heartily sorry for having offended Thee, and I detest all my sins because of Thy just punishments, but most of all because they offend Thee, my God, who art all good and deserving of all my love. I firmly resolve with the help of Thy grace to sin no more and to avoid the near occasion of sin. Amen."

Our Father. Hail Mary. Glory Be.

Session 4 | / / | Source: | Adoration? Y / N

GOD'S PRESENCE

"For where two or three are gathered in my name, I am there among them." – **Matthew 18:20**

Subject *Write or describe the **quotation, scene or event,** or **mystery** that you will meditate on.*

○ SPIRITUAL QUOTATION | ○ SCENE OR EVENT | ○ MYSTERY OF FAITH

MEDITATION

→ **Spiritual quotation:** Read and reread the quotation deliberately and meditatively.

→ **Scene or Event:** Attempt to place yourself into the scene as a participant or as an observer.

→ **Mystery of Faith:** Make comparisons and analogies ("the Kingdom of Heaven is like ...").

Observe *What main ideas or impressions stood out during meditation?*

Reflect *What seems significant about these observations for your life right now?*

Converse *How is God speaking to your heart through this meditation?*

Act *What practical step can you take to bring your meditation to life in your actions today?*

JOURNAL ENTRY

"Draw near to God, and he will draw near to you. Cleanse your hands, you sinners, and purify your hearts, you men of double mind."

JAMES 4:8

EVENING EXAMEN

Examine your conscience about the thoughts, words, deeds, and omissions of this day. Then, with true repentance, pray an **Act of Contrition**: "O my God, I am heartily sorry for having offended Thee, and I detest all my sins because of Thy just punishments, but most of all because they offend Thee, my God, who art all good and deserving of all my love. I firmly resolve with the help of Thy grace to sin no more and to avoid the near occasion of sin. Amen."

Our Father. Hail Mary. Glory Be.

GOD'S PRESENCE

"And remember, I am with you always, to the end of the age." – **Matthew 28:20**

Subject *Write or describe the **quotation, scene or event,** or **mystery** that you will meditate on.*

○ SPIRITUAL QUOTATION | ○ SCENE OR EVENT | ○ MYSTERY OF FAITH

MEDITATION

→ **Spiritual quotation:** Read and reread the quotation deliberately and meditatively.

→ **Scene or Event:** Attempt to place yourself into the scene as a participant or as an observer.

→ **Mystery of Faith:** Make comparisons and analogies ("the Kingdom of Heaven is like ...").

Observe *What main ideas or impressions stood out during meditation?*

Reflect *What seems significant about these observations for your life right now?*

Converse *How is God speaking to your heart through this meditation?*

Act *What practical step can you take to bring your meditation to life in your actions today?*

JOURNAL ENTRY

"Be still before the Lord, and wait patiently for him; do not fret over those who prosper in their way, over those who carry out evil devices."

PSALM 37:7

EVENING EXAMEN

Examine your conscience about the thoughts, words, deeds, and omissions of this day. Then, with true repentance, pray an **Act of Contrition**: "O my God, I am heartily sorry for having offended Thee, and I detest all my sins because of Thy just punishments, but most of all because they offend Thee, my God, who art all good and deserving of all my love. I firmly resolve with the help of Thy grace to sin no more and to avoid the near occasion of sin. Amen."

Our Father. Hail Mary. Glory Be.

Session 6 | / / | Source: | Adoration? Y / N

GOD'S PRESENCE

"The Lord is near to all who call on him, to all who call on him in truth." – **Psalm 145:18**

Subject *Write or describe the **quotation, scene or event,** or **mystery** that you will meditate on.*

○ SPIRITUAL QUOTATION | ○ SCENE OR EVENT | ○ MYSTERY OF FAITH

MEDITATION

→ **Spiritual quotation:** Read and reread the quotation deliberately and meditatively.

→ **Scene or Event:** Attempt to place yourself into the scene as a participant or as an observer.

→ **Mystery of Faith:** Make comparisons and analogies ("the Kingdom of Heaven is like ...").

Observe *What main ideas or impressions stood out during meditation?*

Reflect *What seems significant about these observations for your life right now?*

Converse *How is God speaking to your heart through this meditation?*

Act *What practical step can you take to bring your meditation to life in your actions today?*

JOURNAL ENTRY

"I sought the Lord, and he answered me, and delivered me from all my fears."

PSALM 34:4

EVENING EXAMEN

Examine your conscience about the thoughts, words, deeds, and omissions of this day. Then, with true repentance, pray an **Act of Contrition**: "O my God, I am heartily sorry for having offended Thee, and I detest all my sins because of Thy just punishments, but most of all because they offend Thee, my God, who art all good and deserving of all my love. I firmly resolve with the help of Thy grace to sin no more and to avoid the near occasion of sin. Amen."

Our Father. Hail Mary. Glory Be.

GOD'S PRESENCE

"And he said to him, 'My presence will go with you, and I will give you rest.'" – **Exodus 33:14**

Subject *Write or describe the* ***quotation, scene or event,*** *or* ***mystery*** *that you will meditate on.*

○ SPIRITUAL QUOTATION | ○ SCENE OR EVENT | ○ MYSTERY OF FAITH

MEDITATION

→ **Spiritual quotation:** Read and reread the quotation deliberately and meditatively.

→ **Scene or Event:** Attempt to place yourself into the scene as a participant or as an observer.

→ **Mystery of Faith:** Make comparisons and analogies ("the Kingdom of Heaven is like ...").

Observe *What main ideas or impressions stood out during meditation?*

Reflect *What seems significant about these observations for your life right now?*

Converse *How is God speaking to your heart through this meditation?*

Act *What practical step can you take to bring your meditation to life in your actions today?*

JOURNAL ENTRY

"He who labors as he prays lifts his heart to God with his hands, turning his work into a prayer that glorifies the Creator."

ST. BENEDICT OF NURSIA

EVENING EXAMEN

Examine your conscience about the thoughts, words, deeds, and omissions of this day. Then, with true repentance, pray an **Act of Contrition**: "O my God, I am heartily sorry for having offended Thee, and I detest all my sins because of Thy just punishments, but most of all because they offend Thee, my God, who art all good and deserving of all my love. I firmly resolve with the help of Thy grace to sin no more and to avoid the near occasion of sin. Amen."

Our Father. Hail Mary. Glory Be.

Session 8 | / / | Source: | Adoration? Y / N

GOD'S PRESENCE

"The Lord, your God, is in your midst, a warrior who gives victory; he will rejoice over you with gladness ..." – **Zephaniah 3:17**

Subject *Write or describe the* ***quotation, scene or event,*** *or* ***mystery*** *that you will meditate on.*

○ SPIRITUAL QUOTATION | ○ SCENE OR EVENT | ○ MYSTERY OF FAITH

MEDITATION

→ **Spiritual quotation:** Read and reread the quotation deliberately and meditatively.

→ **Scene or Event:** Attempt to place yourself into the scene as a participant or as an observer.

→ **Mystery of Faith:** Make comparisons and analogies ("the Kingdom of Heaven is like ...").

Observe *What main ideas or impressions stood out during meditation?*

Reflect *What seems significant about these observations for your life right now?*

Converse *How is God speaking to your heart through this meditation?*

Act *What practical step can you take to bring your meditation to life in your actions today?*

JOURNAL ENTRY

"In the silence of the heart God speaks. If you face God in prayer and silence, God will speak to you and guide your path."

ST. TERESA OF CALCUTTA

EVENING EXAMEN

Examine your conscience about the thoughts, words, deeds, and omissions of this day. Then, with true repentance, pray an **Act of Contrition**: "O my God, I am heartily sorry for having offended Thee, and I detest all my sins because of Thy just punishments, but most of all because they offend Thee, my God, who art all good and deserving of all my love. I firmly resolve with the help of Thy grace to sin no more and to avoid the near occasion of sin. Amen."

Our Father. Hail Mary. Glory Be.

Session 9 | / / | Source: | Adoration? Y / N

GOD'S PRESENCE

"The Lord is my shepherd, I shall not want." – **Psalm 23:1**

Subject *Write or describe the* ***quotation, scene or event,*** *or* ***mystery*** *that you will meditate on.*

○ SPIRITUAL QUOTATION | ○ SCENE OR EVENT | ○ MYSTERY OF FAITH

MEDITATION

→ **Spiritual quotation:** Read and reread the quotation deliberately and meditatively.

→ **Scene or Event:** Attempt to place yourself into the scene as a participant or as an observer.

→ **Mystery of Faith:** Make comparisons and analogies ("the Kingdom of Heaven is like ...").

Observe *What main ideas or impressions stood out during meditation?*

Reflect *What seems significant about these observations for your life right now?*

Converse *How is God speaking to your heart through this meditation?*

Act *What practical step can you take to bring your meditation to life in your actions today?*

JOURNAL ENTRY

"Meditation is a close application of the mind to divine truths, enlightening the understanding and inflaming the will towards God."

ST. TERESA OF ÁVILA

EVENING EXAMEN

Examine your conscience about the thoughts, words, deeds, and omissions of this day. Then, with true repentance, pray an **Act of Contrition**: "O my God, I am heartily sorry for having offended Thee, and I detest all my sins because of Thy just punishments, but most of all because they offend Thee, my God, who art all good and deserving of all my love. I firmly resolve with the help of Thy grace to sin no more and to avoid the near occasion of sin. Amen."

Our Father. Hail Mary. Glory Be.

Session 10 | / / | Source: | Adoration? Y / N

GOD'S PRESENCE

"... I will never leave you or forsake you." – **Hebrews 13:5**

Subject *Write or describe the* ***quotation, scene or event,*** *or* ***mystery*** *that you will meditate on.*

○ SPIRITUAL QUOTATION | ○ SCENE OR EVENT | ○ MYSTERY OF FAITH

MEDITATION

→ **Spiritual quotation:** Read and reread the quotation deliberately and meditatively.

→ **Scene or Event:** Attempt to place yourself into the scene as a participant or as an observer.

→ **Mystery of Faith:** Make comparisons and analogies ("the Kingdom of Heaven is like ...").

Observe *What main ideas or impressions stood out during meditation?*

Reflect *What seems significant about these observations for your life right now?*

Converse *How is God speaking to your heart through this meditation?*

Act *What practical step can you take to bring your meditation to life in your actions today?*

JOURNAL ENTRY

"Contemplation is a gaze of faith, fixed on Jesus. 'I look at him and he looks at me': a peasant of Ars on his prayer before the tabernacle."

CATECHISM OF THE CATHOLIC CHURCH 2715

EVENING EXAMEN

Examine your conscience about the thoughts, words, deeds, and omissions of this day. Then, with true repentance, pray an **Act of Contrition**: "O my God, I am heartily sorry for having offended Thee, and I detest all my sins because of Thy just punishments, but most of all because they offend Thee, my God, who art all good and deserving of all my love. I firmly resolve with the help of Thy grace to sin no more and to avoid the near occasion of sin. Amen."

Our Father. Hail Mary. Glory Be.

Session 11 | / / | Source: | Adoration? Y / N

GOD'S PRESENCE

"... Do not fear, for I have redeemed you; I have called you by name, you are mine." – **Isaiah 43:1**

Subject *Write or describe the* ***quotation, scene or event,*** *or* ***mystery*** *that you will meditate on.*

○ SPIRITUAL QUOTATION | ○ SCENE OR EVENT | ○ MYSTERY OF FAITH

MEDITATION

→ **Spiritual quotation:** Read and reread the quotation deliberately and meditatively.

→ **Scene or Event:** Attempt to place yourself into the scene as a participant or as an observer.

→ **Mystery of Faith:** Make comparisons and analogies ("the Kingdom of Heaven is like ...").

Observe *What main ideas or impressions stood out during meditation?*

Reflect *What seems significant about these observations for your life right now?*

Converse *How is God speaking to your heart through this meditation?*

Act *What practical step can you take to bring your meditation to life in your actions today?*

JOURNAL ENTRY

"Do not be afraid to set out on the 'adventure of the Spirit,' which will make you holy and give full meaning to your life in Christ."

POPE BENEDICT XVI

EVENING EXAMEN

Examine your conscience about the thoughts, words, deeds, and omissions of this day. Then, with true repentance, pray an **Act of Contrition**: "O my God, I am heartily sorry for having offended Thee, and I detest all my sins because of Thy just punishments, but most of all because they offend Thee, my God, who art all good and deserving of all my love. I firmly resolve with the help of Thy grace to sin no more and to avoid the near occasion of sin. Amen."

Our Father. Hail Mary. Glory Be.

GOD'S PRESENCE

"Surely God is my salvation; I will trust, and will not be afraid, for the Lord God is my strength and my might ..." – **Isaiah 12:2**

Subject *Write or describe the* ***quotation, scene or event,*** *or* ***mystery*** *that you will meditate on.*

○ SPIRITUAL QUOTATION | ○ SCENE OR EVENT | ○ MYSTERY OF FAITH

MEDITATION

→ **Spiritual quotation:** Read and reread the quotation deliberately and meditatively.

→ **Scene or Event:** Attempt to place yourself into the scene as a participant or as an observer.

→ **Mystery of Faith:** Make comparisons and analogies ("the Kingdom of Heaven is like ...").

Observe *What main ideas or impressions stood out during meditation?*

Reflect *What seems significant about these observations for your life right now?*

Converse *How is God speaking to your heart through this meditation?*

Act *What practical step can you take to bring your meditation to life in your actions today?*

JOURNAL ENTRY

"In prayer, more is accomplished by listening than by talking. Let us leave to God the decisions as to what shall be said, and listen in silence."

ST. FRANCIS DE SALES

EVENING EXAMEN

Examine your conscience about the thoughts, words, deeds, and omissions of this day. Then, with true repentance, pray an **Act of Contrition**: "O my God, I am heartily sorry for having offended Thee, and I detest all my sins because of Thy just punishments, but most of all because they offend Thee, my God, who art all good and deserving of all my love. I firmly resolve with the help of Thy grace to sin no more and to avoid the near occasion of sin. Amen."

Our Father. Hail Mary. Glory Be.

Session 13 | / / | Source: | Adoration? Y / N

GOD'S PRESENCE

"Know that I am with you and will keep you wherever you go, and will bring you back to this land ..." – **Genesis 28:15**

Subject *Write or describe the **quotation, scene or event,** or **mystery** that you will meditate on.*

○ SPIRITUAL QUOTATION | ○ SCENE OR EVENT | ○ MYSTERY OF FAITH

MEDITATION

→ **Spiritual quotation:** Read and reread the quotation deliberately and meditatively.

→ **Scene or Event:** Attempt to place yourself into the scene as a participant or as an observer.

→ **Mystery of Faith:** Make comparisons and analogies ("the Kingdom of Heaven is like ...").

Observe *What main ideas or impressions stood out during meditation?*

Reflect *What seems significant about these observations for your life right now?*

Converse *How is God speaking to your heart through this meditation?*

Act *What practical step can you take to bring your meditation to life in your actions today?*

JOURNAL ENTRY

"Prayer is the inner bath of love into which the soul plunges itself."

ST. JOHN VIANNEY

EVENING EXAMEN

Examine your conscience about the thoughts, words, deeds, and omissions of this day. Then, with true repentance, pray an **Act of Contrition**: "O my God, I am heartily sorry for having offended Thee, and I detest all my sins because of Thy just punishments, but most of all because they offend Thee, my God, who art all good and deserving of all my love. I firmly resolve with the help of Thy grace to sin no more and to avoid the near occasion of sin. Amen."

Our Father. Hail Mary. Glory Be.

Session 14 | / / | Source: | Adoration? Y / N

GOD'S PRESENCE

"God is our refuge and strength, a very present help in trouble." – **Psalm 46:1**

Subject *Write or describe the **quotation, scene or event,** or **mystery** that you will meditate on.*

○ SPIRITUAL QUOTATION | ○ SCENE OR EVENT | ○ MYSTERY OF FAITH

MEDITATION

→ **Spiritual quotation:** Read and reread the quotation deliberately and meditatively.

→ **Scene or Event:** Attempt to place yourself into the scene as a participant or as an observer.

→ **Mystery of Faith:** Make comparisons and analogies ("the Kingdom of Heaven is like ...").

Observe *What main ideas or impressions stood out during meditation?*

Reflect *What seems significant about these observations for your life right now?*

Converse *How is God speaking to your heart through this meditation?*

Act *What practical step can you take to bring your meditation to life in your actions today?*

JOURNAL ENTRY

"To keep a lamp burning, we have to keep putting oil in it."

ST. TERESA OF CALCUTTA

EVENING EXAMEN

Examine your conscience about the thoughts, words, deeds, and omissions of this day. Then, with true repentance, pray an **Act of Contrition**: "O my God, I am heartily sorry for having offended Thee, and I detest all my sins because of Thy just punishments, but most of all because they offend Thee, my God, who art all good and deserving of all my love. I firmly resolve with the help of Thy grace to sin no more and to avoid the near occasion of sin. Amen."

Our Father. Hail Mary. Glory Be.

Session 15 | / / | Source: | Adoration? Y / N

GOD'S PRESENCE

"The Lord is near to the brokenhearted, and saves the crushed in spirit." – **Psalm 34:18**

Subject *Write or describe the* ***quotation, scene or event,*** *or* ***mystery*** *that you will meditate on.*

○ SPIRITUAL QUOTATION | ○ SCENE OR EVENT | ○ MYSTERY OF FAITH

MEDITATION

→ **Spiritual quotation:** Read and reread the quotation deliberately and meditatively.

→ **Scene or Event:** Attempt to place yourself into the scene as a participant or as an observer.

→ **Mystery of Faith:** Make comparisons and analogies ("the Kingdom of Heaven is like ...").

Observe *What main ideas or impressions stood out during meditation?*

Reflect *What seems significant about these observations for your life right now?*

Converse *How is God speaking to your heart through this meditation?*

Act *What practical step can you take to bring your meditation to life in your actions today?*

JOURNAL ENTRY

"God commands you to pray, but He forbids you to worry."

ST. JOHN VIANNEY

EVENING EXAMEN

Examine your conscience about the thoughts, words, deeds, and omissions of this day. Then, with true repentance, pray an **Act of Contrition**: "O my God, I am heartily sorry for having offended Thee, and I detest all my sins because of Thy just punishments, but most of all because they offend Thee, my God, who art all good and deserving of all my love. I firmly resolve with the help of Thy grace to sin no more and to avoid the near occasion of sin. Amen."

Our Father. Hail Mary. Glory Be.

Session 16 | / / | Source: | Adoration? Y / N

GOD'S PRESENCE

"But for me it is good to be near God; I have made the Lord God my refuge ..." – **Psalm 73:28**

Subject *Write or describe the* ***quotation, scene or event,*** *or* ***mystery*** *that you will meditate on.*

○ SPIRITUAL QUOTATION | ○ SCENE OR EVENT | ○ MYSTERY OF FAITH

MEDITATION

→ **Spiritual quotation:** Read and reread the quotation deliberately and meditatively.

→ **Scene or Event:** Attempt to place yourself into the scene as a participant or as an observer.

→ **Mystery of Faith:** Make comparisons and analogies ("the Kingdom of Heaven is like ...").

Observe *What main ideas or impressions stood out during meditation?*

Reflect *What seems significant about these observations for your life right now?*

Converse *How is God speaking to your heart through this meditation?*

Act *What practical step can you take to bring your meditation to life in your actions today?*

JOURNAL ENTRY

"True prayer is neither a mere mental exercise nor a vocal performance. It is far deeper than that—it is spiritual communion with God."

ST. JOHN OF THE CROSS

EVENING EXAMEN

Examine your conscience about the thoughts, words, deeds, and omissions of this day. Then, with true repentance, pray an **Act of Contrition**: "O my God, I am heartily sorry for having offended Thee, and I detest all my sins because of Thy just punishments, but most of all because they offend Thee, my God, who art all good and deserving of all my love. I firmly resolve with the help of Thy grace to sin no more and to avoid the near occasion of sin. Amen."

Our Father. Hail Mary. Glory Be.

GOD'S PRESENCE

"The Lord is my light and my salvation; whom shall I fear?" – **Psalm 27:1**

Subject *Write or describe the* ***quotation, scene or event,*** *or* ***mystery*** *that you will meditate on.*

○ SPIRITUAL QUOTATION | ○ SCENE OR EVENT | ○ MYSTERY OF FAITH

MEDITATION

→ **Spiritual quotation:** Read and reread the quotation deliberately and meditatively.

→ **Scene or Event:** Attempt to place yourself into the scene as a participant or as an observer.

→ **Mystery of Faith:** Make comparisons and analogies ("the Kingdom of Heaven is like ...").

Observe *What main ideas or impressions stood out during meditation?*

Reflect *What seems significant about these observations for your life right now?*

Converse *How is God speaking to your heart through this meditation?*

Act *What practical step can you take to bring your meditation to life in your actions today?*

JOURNAL ENTRY

"Silence is more important than any other human work, for it expresses God. The true revolution comes from silence; it leads us toward God and others."

CARDINAL ROBERT SARAH

EVENING EXAMEN

Examine your conscience about the thoughts, words, deeds, and omissions of this day. Then, with true repentance, pray an **Act of Contrition**: "O my God, I am heartily sorry for having offended Thee, and I detest all my sins because of Thy just punishments, but most of all because they offend Thee, my God, who art all good and deserving of all my love. I firmly resolve with the help of Thy grace to sin no more and to avoid the near occasion of sin. Amen."

Our Father. Hail Mary. Glory Be.

Session 18 | / / | Source: | Adoration? Y / N

GOD'S PRESENCE

"Even though I walk through the darkest valley, I fear no evil; for you are with me ..." – **Psalm 23:4**

Subject *Write or describe the **quotation, scene or event,** or **mystery** that you will meditate on.*

○ SPIRITUAL QUOTATION | ○ SCENE OR EVENT | ○ MYSTERY OF FAITH

MEDITATION

→ **Spiritual quotation:** Read and reread the quotation deliberately and meditatively.

→ **Scene or Event:** Attempt to place yourself into the scene as a participant or as an observer.

→ **Mystery of Faith:** Make comparisons and analogies ("the Kingdom of Heaven is like ...").

Observe *What main ideas or impressions stood out during meditation?*

Reflect *What seems significant about these observations for your life right now?*

Converse *How is God speaking to your heart through this meditation?*

Act *What practical step can you take to bring your meditation to life in your actions today?*

JOURNAL ENTRY

"Nothing is equal to prayer; for what is impossible it makes possible, what is difficult, easy."

ST. JOHN CHRYSOSTOM

EVENING EXAMEN

Examine your conscience about the thoughts, words, deeds, and omissions of this day. Then, with true repentance, pray an **Act of Contrition**: "O my God, I am heartily sorry for having offended Thee, and I detest all my sins because of Thy just punishments, but most of all because they offend Thee, my God, who art all good and deserving of all my love. I firmly resolve with the help of Thy grace to sin no more and to avoid the near occasion of sin. Amen."

Our Father. Hail Mary. Glory Be.

Session 19 | / / | Source: | Adoration? Y / N

GOD'S PRESENCE

"When you search for me, you will find me; if you seek me with all your heart." – **Jeremiah 29:13**

Subject *Write or describe the* ***quotation, scene or event,*** *or* ***mystery*** *that you will meditate on.*

○ SPIRITUAL QUOTATION | ○ SCENE OR EVENT | ○ MYSTERY OF FAITH

MEDITATION

→ **Spiritual quotation:** Read and reread the quotation deliberately and meditatively.

→ **Scene or Event:** Attempt to place yourself into the scene as a participant or as an observer.

→ **Mystery of Faith:** Make comparisons and analogies ("the Kingdom of Heaven is like ...").

Observe *What main ideas or impressions stood out during meditation?*

Reflect *What seems significant about these observations for your life right now?*

Converse *How is God speaking to your heart through this meditation?*

Act *What practical step can you take to bring your meditation to life in your actions today?*

JOURNAL ENTRY

"Acquire the habit of speaking to God as if you were alone with Him, familiarly and with ... love, as to the dearest and most loving of friends."

ST. ALPHONSUS LIGUORI

EVENING EXAMEN

Examine your conscience about the thoughts, words, deeds, and omissions of this day. Then, with true repentance, pray an **Act of Contrition**: "O my God, I am heartily sorry for having offended Thee, and I detest all my sins because of Thy just punishments, but most of all because they offend Thee, my God, who art all good and deserving of all my love. I firmly resolve with the help of Thy grace to sin no more and to avoid the near occasion of sin. Amen."

Our Father. Hail Mary. Glory Be.

Session 20 | / / | Source: | Adoration? Y / N

GOD'S PRESENCE

"Draw near to God, and he will draw near to you ..." – **James 4:8**

Subject *Write or describe the* ***quotation, scene or event,*** *or* ***mystery*** *that you will meditate on.*

○ SPIRITUAL QUOTATION | ○ SCENE OR EVENT | ○ MYSTERY OF FAITH

MEDITATION

→ **Spiritual quotation:** Read and reread the quotation deliberately and meditatively.

→ **Scene or Event:** Attempt to place yourself into the scene as a participant or as an observer.

→ **Mystery of Faith:** Make comparisons and analogies ("the Kingdom of Heaven is like ...").

Observe *What main ideas or impressions stood out during meditation?*

Reflect *What seems significant about these observations for your life right now?*

Converse *How is God speaking to your heart through this meditation?*

Act *What practical step can you take to bring your meditation to life in your actions today?*

JOURNAL ENTRY

"If you are seeking God but do not know where to begin, learn to pray and make that your habit."

ST. TERESA OF ÁVILA

EVENING EXAMEN

Examine your conscience about the thoughts, words, deeds, and omissions of this day. Then, with true repentance, pray an **Act of Contrition**: "O my God, I am heartily sorry for having offended Thee, and I detest all my sins because of Thy just punishments, but most of all because they offend Thee, my God, who art all good and deserving of all my love. I firmly resolve with the help of Thy grace to sin no more and to avoid the near occasion of sin. Amen."

Our Father. Hail Mary. Glory Be.

Session 21 | / / | Source: | Adoration? Y / N

GOD'S PRESENCE

"The Lord of hosts is with us; the God of Jacob is our refuge." – **Psalm 46:7**

Subject *Write or describe the **quotation, scene or event,** or **mystery** that you will meditate on.*

○ SPIRITUAL QUOTATION | ○ SCENE OR EVENT | ○ MYSTERY OF FAITH

MEDITATION

→ **Spiritual quotation:** Read and reread the quotation deliberately and meditatively.

→ **Scene or Event:** Attempt to place yourself into the scene as a participant or as an observer.

→ **Mystery of Faith:** Make comparisons and analogies ("the Kingdom of Heaven is like ...").

Observe *What main ideas or impressions stood out during meditation?*

Reflect *What seems significant about these observations for your life right now?*

Converse *How is God speaking to your heart through this meditation?*

Act *What practical step can you take to bring your meditation to life in your actions today?*

JOURNAL ENTRY

"To meditate on the law of the Lord is an excellent way to find inner peace and guidance from the Holy Spirit."

ST. THOMAS AQUINAS

EVENING EXAMEN

Examine your conscience about the thoughts, words, deeds, and omissions of this day. Then, with true repentance, pray an **Act of Contrition**: "O my God, I am heartily sorry for having offended Thee, and I detest all my sins because of Thy just punishments, but most of all because they offend Thee, my God, who art all good and deserving of all my love. I firmly resolve with the help of Thy grace to sin no more and to avoid the near occasion of sin. Amen."

Our Father. Hail Mary. Glory Be.

Session 22 | / / | Source: | Adoration? Y / N

GOD'S PRESENCE

"The eternal God is your dwelling place, and underneath are the everlasting arms ..." – **Deuteronomy 33:27**

Subject *Write or describe the* ***quotation, scene or event,*** *or* ***mystery*** *that you will meditate on.*

○ SPIRITUAL QUOTATION | ○ SCENE OR EVENT | ○ MYSTERY OF FAITH

MEDITATION

→ **Spiritual quotation:** Read and reread the quotation deliberately and meditatively.

→ **Scene or Event:** Attempt to place yourself into the scene as a participant or as an observer.

→ **Mystery of Faith:** Make comparisons and analogies ("the Kingdom of Heaven is like ...").

Observe *What main ideas or impressions stood out during meditation?*

Reflect *What seems significant about these observations for your life right now?*

Converse *How is God speaking to your heart through this meditation?*

Act *What practical step can you take to bring your meditation to life in your actions today?*

JOURNAL ENTRY

"Let prayer be our soul's breath, and meditation our daily bread."

ST. JOHN DAMASCENE

EVENING EXAMEN

Examine your conscience about the thoughts, words, deeds, and omissions of this day. Then, with true repentance, pray an **Act of Contrition**: "O my God, I am heartily sorry for having offended Thee, and I detest all my sins because of Thy just punishments, but most of all because they offend Thee, my God, who art all good and deserving of all my love. I firmly resolve with the help of Thy grace to sin no more and to avoid the near occasion of sin. Amen."

Our Father. Hail Mary. Glory Be.

GOD'S PRESENCE

"You show me the path of life. In your presence there is fullness of joy ..." – **Psalm 16:11**

Subject *Write or describe the **quotation, scene or event,** or **mystery** that you will meditate on.*

○ SPIRITUAL QUOTATION | ○ SCENE OR EVENT | ○ MYSTERY OF FAITH

MEDITATION

→ **Spiritual quotation:** Read and reread the quotation deliberately and meditatively.

→ **Scene or Event:** Attempt to place yourself into the scene as a participant or as an observer.

→ **Mystery of Faith:** Make comparisons and analogies ("the Kingdom of Heaven is like ...").

Observe *What main ideas or impressions stood out during meditation?*

Reflect *What seems significant about these observations for your life right now?*

Converse *How is God speaking to your heart through this meditation?*

Act *What practical step can you take to bring your meditation to life in your actions today?*

JOURNAL ENTRY

"The more we pray, the more we invite the Holy Spirit into our lives, allowing us to be shaped and formed by God's will."

ST. CATHERINE OF SIENA

EVENING EXAMEN

Examine your conscience about the thoughts, words, deeds, and omissions of this day. Then, with true repentance, pray an **Act of Contrition**: "O my God, I am heartily sorry for having offended Thee, and I detest all my sins because of Thy just punishments, but most of all because they offend Thee, my God, who art all good and deserving of all my love. I firmly resolve with the help of Thy grace to sin no more and to avoid the near occasion of sin. Amen."

Our Father. Hail Mary. Glory Be.

GOD'S PRESENCE

"You who live in the shelter of the Most High, who abide in the shadow of the Almighty ..." – **Psalm 91:1**

Subject *Write or describe the* ***quotation, scene or event,*** *or* ***mystery*** *that you will meditate on.*

○ SPIRITUAL QUOTATION | ○ SCENE OR EVENT | ○ MYSTERY OF FAITH

MEDITATION

→ **Spiritual quotation:** Read and reread the quotation deliberately and meditatively.

→ **Scene or Event:** Attempt to place yourself into the scene as a participant or as an observer.

→ **Mystery of Faith:** Make comparisons and analogies ("the Kingdom of Heaven is like ...").

Observe *What main ideas or impressions stood out during meditation?*

Reflect *What seems significant about these observations for your life right now?*

Converse *How is God speaking to your heart through this meditation?*

Act *What practical step can you take to bring your meditation to life in your actions today?*

JOURNAL ENTRY

"Meditation on the sufferings of Christ will show you the depth of His love for you, and will guide you on the path to sanctity."

ST. BONAVENTURE

EVENING EXAMEN

Examine your conscience about the thoughts, words, deeds, and omissions of this day. Then, with true repentance, pray an **Act of Contrition**: "O my God, I am heartily sorry for having offended Thee, and I detest all my sins because of Thy just punishments, but most of all because they offend Thee, my God, who art all good and deserving of all my love. I firmly resolve with the help of Thy grace to sin no more and to avoid the near occasion of sin. Amen."

Our Father. Hail Mary. Glory Be.

Session 25 | / / | Source: | Adoration? Y / N

GOD'S PRESENCE

"Then Jacob woke from his sleep and said, 'Surely the Lord is in this place—and I did not know it!'" – **Genesis 28:16**

Subject *Write or describe the* ***quotation, scene or event,*** *or* ***mystery*** *that you will meditate on.*

○ SPIRITUAL QUOTATION | ○ SCENE OR EVENT | ○ MYSTERY OF FAITH

MEDITATION

→ **Spiritual quotation:** Read and reread the quotation deliberately and meditatively.

→ **Scene or Event:** Attempt to place yourself into the scene as a participant or as an observer.

→ **Mystery of Faith:** Make comparisons and analogies ("the Kingdom of Heaven is like ...").

Observe *What main ideas or impressions stood out during meditation?*

Reflect *What seems significant about these observations for your life right now?*

Converse *How is God speaking to your heart through this meditation?*

Act *What practical step can you take to bring your meditation to life in your actions today?*

JOURNAL ENTRY

"In the stillness of prayer, the soul finds its true home in the heart of Christ."

ST. ELIZABETH ANN SETON

EVENING EXAMEN

Examine your conscience about the thoughts, words, deeds, and omissions of this day. Then, with true repentance, pray an **Act of Contrition**: "O my God, I am heartily sorry for having offended Thee, and I detest all my sins because of Thy just punishments, but most of all because they offend Thee, my God, who art all good and deserving of all my love. I firmly resolve with the help of Thy grace to sin no more and to avoid the near occasion of sin. Amen."

Our Father. Hail Mary. Glory Be.

Session 26 | / / | Source: | Adoration? Y / N

GOD'S PRESENCE

"Abide in me as I abide in you. Just as the branch cannot bear fruit by itself unless it abides in the vine ..." **– John 15:4**

Subject *Write or describe the **quotation, scene or event,** or **mystery** that you will meditate on.*

○ SPIRITUAL QUOTATION | ○ SCENE OR EVENT | ○ MYSTERY OF FAITH

MEDITATION

→ **Spiritual quotation:** Read and reread the quotation deliberately and meditatively.

→ **Scene or Event:** Attempt to place yourself into the scene as a participant or as an observer.

→ **Mystery of Faith:** Make comparisons and analogies ("the Kingdom of Heaven is like ...").

Observe *What main ideas or impressions stood out during meditation?*

Reflect *What seems significant about these observations for your life right now?*

Converse *How is God speaking to your heart through this meditation?*

Act *What practical step can you take to bring your meditation to life in your actions today?*

JOURNAL ENTRY

"Even when God seems silent, He speaks to us through the desires of our hearts and the peace found in quiet meditation."

ST. IGNATIUS OF LOYOLA

EVENING EXAMEN

Examine your conscience about the thoughts, words, deeds, and omissions of this day. Then, with true repentance, pray an **Act of Contrition**: "O my God, I am heartily sorry for having offended Thee, and I detest all my sins because of Thy just punishments, but most of all because they offend Thee, my God, who art all good and deserving of all my love. I firmly resolve with the help of Thy grace to sin no more and to avoid the near occasion of sin. Amen."

Our Father. Hail Mary. Glory Be.

Session 27 | / / | Source: | Adoration? Y / N

GOD'S PRESENCE

"For I, the Lord your God, hold your right hand; it is I who say to you, 'Do not fear, I will help you.'" – **Isaiah 41:13**

Subject *Write or describe the **quotation, scene or event,** or **mystery** that you will meditate on.*

○ SPIRITUAL QUOTATION | ○ SCENE OR EVENT | ○ MYSTERY OF FAITH

MEDITATION

→ **Spiritual quotation:** Read and reread the quotation deliberately and meditatively.

→ **Scene or Event:** Attempt to place yourself into the scene as a participant or as an observer.

→ **Mystery of Faith:** Make comparisons and analogies ("the Kingdom of Heaven is like ...").

Observe *What main ideas or impressions stood out during meditation?*

Reflect *What seems significant about these observations for your life right now?*

Converse *How is God speaking to your heart through this meditation?*

Act *What practical step can you take to bring your meditation to life in your actions today?*

JOURNAL ENTRY

"Prayer and meditation form the wings of the soul; without them, we cannot reach heaven."

ST. AUGUSTINE OF HIPPO

EVENING EXAMEN

Examine your conscience about the thoughts, words, deeds, and omissions of this day. Then, with true repentance, pray an **Act of Contrition**: "O my God, I am heartily sorry for having offended Thee, and I detest all my sins because of Thy just punishments, but most of all because they offend Thee, my God, who art all good and deserving of all my love. I firmly resolve with the help of Thy grace to sin no more and to avoid the near occasion of sin. Amen."

Our Father. Hail Mary. Glory Be.

Session 28 | / / | Source: | Adoration? Y / N

GOD'S PRESENCE

"The Lord is good to those who wait for him, to the soul that seeks him." – **Lamentations 3:25**

Subject *Write or describe the* ***quotation, scene or event,*** *or* ***mystery*** *that you will meditate on.*

○ SPIRITUAL QUOTATION | ○ SCENE OR EVENT | ○ MYSTERY OF FAITH

MEDITATION

→ **Spiritual quotation:** Read and reread the quotation deliberately and meditatively.

→ **Scene or Event:** Attempt to place yourself into the scene as a participant or as an observer.

→ **Mystery of Faith:** Make comparisons and analogies ("the Kingdom of Heaven is like ...").

Observe *What main ideas or impressions stood out during meditation?*

Reflect *What seems significant about these observations for your life right now?*

Converse *How is God speaking to your heart through this meditation?*

Act *What practical step can you take to bring your meditation to life in your actions today?*

JOURNAL ENTRY

"In your prayer, offer everything to God—your successes and failures, joys and sorrows, so that He may transform them into grace."

ST. THÉRÈSE OF LISIEUX

EVENING EXAMEN

Examine your conscience about the thoughts, words, deeds, and omissions of this day. Then, with true repentance, pray an **Act of Contrition**: "O my God, I am heartily sorry for having offended Thee, and I detest all my sins because of Thy just punishments, but most of all because they offend Thee, my God, who art all good and deserving of all my love. I firmly resolve with the help of Thy grace to sin no more and to avoid the near occasion of sin. Amen."

Our Father. Hail Mary. Glory Be.

GOD'S PRESENCE

"The Lord will fight for you, and you have only to keep still." – **Exodus 14:14**

Subject *Write or describe the* ***quotation, scene or event,*** *or* ***mystery*** *that you will meditate on.*

○ SPIRITUAL QUOTATION | ○ SCENE OR EVENT | ○ MYSTERY OF FAITH

MEDITATION

→ **Spiritual quotation:** Read and reread the quotation deliberately and meditatively.

→ **Scene or Event:** Attempt to place yourself into the scene as a participant or as an observer.

→ **Mystery of Faith:** Make comparisons and analogies ("the Kingdom of Heaven is like ...").

Observe *What main ideas or impressions stood out during meditation?*

Reflect *What seems significant about these observations for your life right now?*

Converse *How is God speaking to your heart through this meditation?*

Act *What practical step can you take to bring your meditation to life in your actions today?*

JOURNAL ENTRY

"Let your meditation be a preparation for meeting God face to face. Pray to understand His will and to conform yourself to it."

ST. FRANCIS OF ASSISI

EVENING EXAMEN

Examine your conscience about the thoughts, words, deeds, and omissions of this day. Then, with true repentance, pray an **Act of Contrition**: "O my God, I am heartily sorry for having offended Thee, and I detest all my sins because of Thy just punishments, but most of all because they offend Thee, my God, who art all good and deserving of all my love. I firmly resolve with the help of Thy grace to sin no more and to avoid the near occasion of sin. Amen."

Our Father. Hail Mary. Glory Be.

Session 30 | / / | Source: | Adoration? Y / N

GOD'S PRESENCE

"The Lord is gracious and merciful, slow to anger and abounding in steadfast love." – **Psalm 145:8**

Subject *Write or describe the* ***quotation, scene or event,*** *or* ***mystery*** *that you will meditate on.*

○ SPIRITUAL QUOTATION | ○ SCENE OR EVENT | ○ MYSTERY OF FAITH

MEDITATION

→ **Spiritual quotation:** Read and reread the quotation deliberately and meditatively.

→ **Scene or Event:** Attempt to place yourself into the scene as a participant or as an observer.

→ **Mystery of Faith:** Make comparisons and analogies ("the Kingdom of Heaven is like ...").

Observe *What main ideas or impressions stood out during meditation?*

Reflect *What seems significant about these observations for your life right now?*

Converse *How is God speaking to your heart through this meditation?*

Act *What practical step can you take to bring your meditation to life in your actions today?*

JOURNAL ENTRY

"The highest form of prayer is to stand silently in awe before God."

ST. IGNATIUS OF LOYOLA

EVENING EXAMEN

Examine your conscience about the thoughts, words, deeds, and omissions of this day. Then, with true repentance, pray an **Act of Contrition**: "O my God, I am heartily sorry for having offended Thee, and I detest all my sins because of Thy just punishments, but most of all because they offend Thee, my God, who art all good and deserving of all my love. I firmly resolve with the help of Thy grace to sin no more and to avoid the near occasion of sin. Amen."

Our Father. Hail Mary. Glory Be.

MONTH 2

YOUR RELATIONSHIP WITH GOD

By now, your meditation practice is beginning to bear fruit. This month, focus on deepening your relationship with God, listening to His voice, and allowing Him to shape your heart more fully. Reflect on the ways God is drawing you closer.

How has your image of God changed since you began meditating daily?

What specific areas of your life is God calling you to surrender to Him?

How has meditation helped you rely more on God's guidance in difficulty?

What does it mean to listen to God during prayer, rather than just speaking?

How has meditation transformed your approach to spiritual growth?

Session 31 | / / | Source: | Adoration? Y / N

GOD'S PRESENCE

"For 'In him we live and move and have our being'; as even some of your own poets have said ..." – **Acts 17:28**

Subject *Write or describe the **quotation, scene or event,** or **mystery** that you will meditate on.*

○ SPIRITUAL QUOTATION | ○ SCENE OR EVENT | ○ MYSTERY OF FAITH

MEDITATION

→ **Spiritual quotation:** Read and reread the quotation deliberately and meditatively.

→ **Scene or Event:** Attempt to place yourself into the scene as a participant or as an observer.

→ **Mystery of Faith:** Make comparisons and analogies ("the Kingdom of Heaven is like ...").

Observe *What main ideas or impressions stood out during meditation?*

Reflect *What seems significant about these observations for your life right now?*

Converse *How is God speaking to your heart through this meditation?*

Act *What practical step can you take to bring your meditation to life in your actions today?*

JOURNAL ENTRY

"Rejoice always, pray constantly, give thanks in all circumstances; for this is the will of God in Christ Jesus for you."

1 THESSALONIANS 5:16-18

EVENING EXAMEN

Examine your conscience about the thoughts, words, deeds, and omissions of this day. Then, with true repentance, pray an **Act of Contrition**: "O my God, I am heartily sorry for having offended Thee, and I detest all my sins because of Thy just punishments, but most of all because they offend Thee, my God, who art all good and deserving of all my love. I firmly resolve with the help of Thy grace to sin no more and to avoid the near occasion of sin. Amen."

Our Father. Hail Mary. Glory Be.

Session 32 | / / | Source: | Adoration? Y / N

GOD'S PRESENCE

"And the peace of God, which surpasses all understanding, will guard your hearts and your minds." – **Philippians 4:7**

Subject *Write or describe the* ***quotation, scene or event,*** *or* ***mystery*** *that you will meditate on.*

○ SPIRITUAL QUOTATION | ○ SCENE OR EVENT | ○ MYSTERY OF FAITH

MEDITATION

→ **Spiritual quotation:** Read and reread the quotation deliberately and meditatively.

→ **Scene or Event:** Attempt to place yourself into the scene as a participant or as an observer.

→ **Mystery of Faith:** Make comparisons and analogies ("the Kingdom of Heaven is like ...").

Observe *What main ideas or impressions stood out during meditation?*

Reflect *What seems significant about these observations for your life right now?*

Converse *How is God speaking to your heart through this meditation?*

Act *What practical step can you take to bring your meditation to life in your actions today?*

JOURNAL ENTRY

"Seek the Lord and his strength, seek his presence continually!"

1 CHRONICLES 16:11

EVENING EXAMEN

Examine your conscience about the thoughts, words, deeds, and omissions of this day. Then, with true repentance, pray an **Act of Contrition**: "O my God, I am heartily sorry for having offended Thee, and I detest all my sins because of Thy just punishments, but most of all because they offend Thee, my God, who art all good and deserving of all my love. I firmly resolve with the help of Thy grace to sin no more and to avoid the near occasion of sin. Amen."

Our Father. Hail Mary. Glory Be.

Session 33 | / / | Source: | Adoration? Y / N

GOD'S PRESENCE

"... In everything by prayer and supplication with thanksgiving let your requests be made known to God." – **Philippians 4:6**

Subject *Write or describe the* ***quotation, scene or event,*** *or* ***mystery*** *that you will meditate on.*

○ SPIRITUAL QUOTATION | ○ SCENE OR EVENT | ○ MYSTERY OF FAITH

MEDITATION

→ **Spiritual quotation:** Read and reread the quotation deliberately and meditatively.

→ **Scene or Event:** Attempt to place yourself into the scene as a participant or as an observer.

→ **Mystery of Faith:** Make comparisons and analogies ("the Kingdom of Heaven is like ...").

Observe *What main ideas or impressions stood out during meditation?*

Reflect *What seems significant about these observations for your life right now?*

Converse *How is God speaking to your heart through this meditation?*

Act *What practical step can you take to bring your meditation to life in your actions today?*

JOURNAL ENTRY

"The Lord is near to all who call upon him, to all who call upon him in truth."

PSALM 145:18

EVENING EXAMEN

Examine your conscience about the thoughts, words, deeds, and omissions of this day. Then, with true repentance, pray an **Act of Contrition**: "O my God, I am heartily sorry for having offended Thee, and I detest all my sins because of Thy just punishments, but most of all because they offend Thee, my God, who art all good and deserving of all my love. I firmly resolve with the help of Thy grace to sin no more and to avoid the near occasion of sin. Amen."

Our Father. Hail Mary. Glory Be.

Session 34 | / / | Source: | Adoration? Y / N

GOD'S PRESENCE

"I sought the Lord, and he answered me, and delivered me from all my fears." – **Psalm 34:4**

Subject *Write or describe the* ***quotation, scene or event,*** *or* ***mystery*** *that you will meditate on.*

○ SPIRITUAL QUOTATION | ○ SCENE OR EVENT | ○ MYSTERY OF FAITH

MEDITATION

→ **Spiritual quotation:** Read and reread the quotation deliberately and meditatively.

→ **Scene or Event:** Attempt to place yourself into the scene as a participant or as an observer.

→ **Mystery of Faith:** Make comparisons and analogies ("the Kingdom of Heaven is like ...").

Observe *What main ideas or impressions stood out during meditation?*

Reflect *What seems significant about these observations for your life right now?*

Converse *How is God speaking to your heart through this meditation?*

Act *What practical step can you take to bring your meditation to life in your actions today?*

JOURNAL ENTRY

"By prayer we can build a defense against the attacks of the devil, for the devil fears a soul united to God in prayer."

ST. JOHN CHRYSOSTOM

EVENING EXAMEN

Examine your conscience about the thoughts, words, deeds, and omissions of this day. Then, with true repentance, pray an **Act of Contrition**: "O my God, I am heartily sorry for having offended Thee, and I detest all my sins because of Thy just punishments, but most of all because they offend Thee, my God, who art all good and deserving of all my love. I firmly resolve with the help of Thy grace to sin no more and to avoid the near occasion of sin. Amen."

Our Father. Hail Mary. Glory Be.

GOD'S PRESENCE

"The steadfast love of the Lord never ceases, his mercies never come to an end ..." – **Lamentations 3:22**

Subject *Write or describe the* ***quotation, scene or event,*** *or* ***mystery*** *that you will meditate on.*

○ SPIRITUAL QUOTATION | ○ SCENE OR EVENT | ○ MYSTERY OF FAITH

MEDITATION

→ **Spiritual quotation:** Read and reread the quotation deliberately and meditatively.

→ **Scene or Event:** Attempt to place yourself into the scene as a participant or as an observer.

→ **Mystery of Faith:** Make comparisons and analogies ("the Kingdom of Heaven is like ...").

Observe *What main ideas or impressions stood out during meditation?*

Reflect *What seems significant about these observations for your life right now?*

Converse *How is God speaking to your heart through this meditation?*

Act *What practical step can you take to bring your meditation to life in your actions today?*

JOURNAL ENTRY

"Let us not forget to offer each day, with our morning prayers, our work, sufferings, and joys, for the love of Christ."

ST. THÉRÈSE OF LISIEUX

EVENING EXAMEN

Examine your conscience about the thoughts, words, deeds, and omissions of this day. Then, with true repentance, pray an **Act of Contrition**: "O my God, I am heartily sorry for having offended Thee, and I detest all my sins because of Thy just punishments, but most of all because they offend Thee, my God, who art all good and deserving of all my love. I firmly resolve with the help of Thy grace to sin no more and to avoid the near occasion of sin. Amen."

Our Father. Hail Mary. Glory Be.

Session 36 | / / | Source: | Adoration? Y / N

GOD'S PRESENCE

"Come to me, all you that are weary and are carrying heavy burdens, and I will give you rest." – **Matthew 11:28**

Subject *Write or describe the* ***quotation, scene or event,*** *or* ***mystery*** *that you will meditate on.*

○ SPIRITUAL QUOTATION | ○ SCENE OR EVENT | ○ MYSTERY OF FAITH

MEDITATION

→ **Spiritual quotation:** Read and reread the quotation deliberately and meditatively.

→ **Scene or Event:** Attempt to place yourself into the scene as a participant or as an observer.

→ **Mystery of Faith:** Make comparisons and analogies ("the Kingdom of Heaven is like ...").

Observe *What main ideas or impressions stood out during meditation?*

Reflect *What seems significant about these observations for your life right now?*

Converse *How is God speaking to your heart through this meditation?*

Act *What practical step can you take to bring your meditation to life in your actions today?*

JOURNAL ENTRY

"It is not so much the length of prayer, but the fervor and humility with which it is said that pleases God."

ST. FRANCIS DE SALES

EVENING EXAMEN

Examine your conscience about the thoughts, words, deeds, and omissions of this day. Then, with true repentance, pray an **Act of Contrition**: "O my God, I am heartily sorry for having offended Thee, and I detest all my sins because of Thy just punishments, but most of all because they offend Thee, my God, who art all good and deserving of all my love. I firmly resolve with the help of Thy grace to sin no more and to avoid the near occasion of sin. Amen."

Our Father. Hail Mary. Glory Be.

Session 37 | / / | Source: | Adoration? Y / N

GOD'S PRESENCE

"Be strong and bold; have no fear or dread ... because it is the Lord your God who goes with you ..." **– Deuteronomy 31:6**

Subject *Write or describe the* ***quotation, scene or event,*** *or* ***mystery*** *that you will meditate on.*

○ SPIRITUAL QUOTATION | ○ SCENE OR EVENT | ○ MYSTERY OF FAITH

MEDITATION

→ **Spiritual quotation:** Read and reread the quotation deliberately and meditatively.

→ **Scene or Event:** Attempt to place yourself into the scene as a participant or as an observer.

→ **Mystery of Faith:** Make comparisons and analogies ("the Kingdom of Heaven is like ...").

Observe *What main ideas or impressions stood out during meditation?*

Reflect *What seems significant about these observations for your life right now?*

Converse *How is God speaking to your heart through this meditation?*

Act *What practical step can you take to bring your meditation to life in your actions today?*

JOURNAL ENTRY

"God has created us to love and to be loved, and this is the beginning of prayer—knowing that He loves us, that we are precious to Him."

ST. TERESA OF CALCUTTA

EVENING EXAMEN

Examine your conscience about the thoughts, words, deeds, and omissions of this day. Then, with true repentance, pray an **Act of Contrition**: "O my God, I am heartily sorry for having offended Thee, and I detest all my sins because of Thy just punishments, but most of all because they offend Thee, my God, who art all good and deserving of all my love. I firmly resolve with the help of Thy grace to sin no more and to avoid the near occasion of sin. Amen."

Our Father. Hail Mary. Glory Be.

GOD'S PRESENCE

"The Lord is my strength and my shield; in him my heart trusts ..." – **Psalm 28:7**

Subject *Write or describe the* ***quotation, scene or event,*** *or* ***mystery*** *that you will meditate on.*

○ SPIRITUAL QUOTATION | ○ SCENE OR EVENT | ○ MYSTERY OF FAITH

MEDITATION

→ **Spiritual quotation:** Read and reread the quotation deliberately and meditatively.

→ **Scene or Event:** Attempt to place yourself into the scene as a participant or as an observer.

→ **Mystery of Faith:** Make comparisons and analogies ("the Kingdom of Heaven is like ...").

Observe *What main ideas or impressions stood out during meditation?*

Reflect *What seems significant about these observations for your life right now?*

Converse *How is God speaking to your heart through this meditation?*

Act *What practical step can you take to bring your meditation to life in your actions today?*

JOURNAL ENTRY

"In prayer, we must not only ask for what we desire, but also for the grace to be able to desire what pleases God."

ST. THOMAS AQUINAS

EVENING EXAMEN

Examine your conscience about the thoughts, words, deeds, and omissions of this day. Then, with true repentance, pray an **Act of Contrition**: "O my God, I am heartily sorry for having offended Thee, and I detest all my sins because of Thy just punishments, but most of all because they offend Thee, my God, who art all good and deserving of all my love. I firmly resolve with the help of Thy grace to sin no more and to avoid the near occasion of sin. Amen."

Our Father. Hail Mary. Glory Be.

Session 39 | / / | Source: | Adoration? Y / N

GOD'S PRESENCE

"Cast your burden on the Lord, and he will sustain you; he will never permit the righteous to be moved." – **Psalm 55:22**

Subject *Write or describe the* ***quotation, scene or event,*** *or* ***mystery*** *that you will meditate on.*

○ SPIRITUAL QUOTATION | ○ SCENE OR EVENT | ○ MYSTERY OF FAITH

MEDITATION

→ **Spiritual quotation:** Read and reread the quotation deliberately and meditatively.

→ **Scene or Event:** Attempt to place yourself into the scene as a participant or as an observer.

→ **Mystery of Faith:** Make comparisons and analogies ("the Kingdom of Heaven is like ...").

Observe *What main ideas or impressions stood out during meditation?*

Reflect *What seems significant about these observations for your life right now?*

Converse *How is God speaking to your heart through this meditation?*

Act *What practical step can you take to bring your meditation to life in your actions today?*

JOURNAL ENTRY

"God does not give Himself wholly to us until He sees that we are giving ourselves wholly to Him."

ST. TERESA OF ÁVILA

EVENING EXAMEN

Examine your conscience about the thoughts, words, deeds, and omissions of this day. Then, with true repentance, pray an **Act of Contrition**: "O my God, I am heartily sorry for having offended Thee, and I detest all my sins because of Thy just punishments, but most of all because they offend Thee, my God, who art all good and deserving of all my love. I firmly resolve with the help of Thy grace to sin no more and to avoid the near occasion of sin. Amen."

Our Father. Hail Mary. Glory Be.

Session 40 | / / | Source: | Adoration? Y / N

GOD'S PRESENCE

"When you pass through the waters, I will be with you; and through the rivers, they shall not overwhelm you ..." – **Isaiah 43:2**

Subject *Write or describe the* ***quotation, scene or event,*** *or* ***mystery*** *that you will meditate on.*

○ SPIRITUAL QUOTATION | ○ SCENE OR EVENT | ○ MYSTERY OF FAITH

MEDITATION

→ **Spiritual quotation:** Read and reread the quotation deliberately and meditatively.

→ **Scene or Event:** Attempt to place yourself into the scene as a participant or as an observer.

→ **Mystery of Faith:** Make comparisons and analogies ("the Kingdom of Heaven is like ...").

Observe *What main ideas or impressions stood out during meditation?*

Reflect *What seems significant about these observations for your life right now?*

Converse *How is God speaking to your heart through this meditation?*

Act *What practical step can you take to bring your meditation to life in your actions today?*

JOURNAL ENTRY

"Holiness is not the luxury of the few, it is a simple duty for you and for me."

ST. TERESA OF CALCUTTA

EVENING EXAMEN

Examine your conscience about the thoughts, words, deeds, and omissions of this day. Then, with true repentance, pray an **Act of Contrition**: "O my God, I am heartily sorry for having offended Thee, and I detest all my sins because of Thy just punishments, but most of all because they offend Thee, my God, who art all good and deserving of all my love. I firmly resolve with the help of Thy grace to sin no more and to avoid the near occasion of sin. Amen."

Our Father. Hail Mary. Glory Be.

Session 41 | / / | Source: | Adoration? Y / N

GOD'S PRESENCE

"The Lord is good, a stronghold in a day of trouble; he protects those who take refuge in him." **– Nahum 1:7**

Subject *Write or describe the **quotation, scene or event,** or **mystery** that you will meditate on.*

○ SPIRITUAL QUOTATION | ○ SCENE OR EVENT | ○ MYSTERY OF FAITH

MEDITATION

→ **Spiritual quotation:** Read and reread the quotation deliberately and meditatively.

→ **Scene or Event:** Attempt to place yourself into the scene as a participant or as an observer.

→ **Mystery of Faith:** Make comparisons and analogies ("the Kingdom of Heaven is like ...").

Observe *What main ideas or impressions stood out during meditation?*

Reflect *What seems significant about these observations for your life right now?*

Converse *How is God speaking to your heart through this meditation?*

Act *What practical step can you take to bring your meditation to life in your actions today?*

JOURNAL ENTRY

"Our soul, by means of prayer, is able to approach God with great confidence and intimacy."

ST. CATHERINE OF SIENA

EVENING EXAMEN

Examine your conscience about the thoughts, words, deeds, and omissions of this day. Then, with true repentance, pray an **Act of Contrition**: "O my God, I am heartily sorry for having offended Thee, and I detest all my sins because of Thy just punishments, but most of all because they offend Thee, my God, who art all good and deserving of all my love. I firmly resolve with the help of Thy grace to sin no more and to avoid the near occasion of sin. Amen."

Our Father. Hail Mary. Glory Be.

Session 42 | / / | Source: | Adoration? Y / N

GOD'S PRESENCE

"Even to your old age I am he, even when you turn gray I will carry you. I have made, and I will bear ..." **– Isaiah 46:4**

Subject *Write or describe the* ***quotation, scene or event,*** *or* ***mystery*** *that you will meditate on.*

○ SPIRITUAL QUOTATION | ○ SCENE OR EVENT | ○ MYSTERY OF FAITH

MEDITATION

→ **Spiritual quotation:** Read and reread the quotation deliberately and meditatively.

→ **Scene or Event:** Attempt to place yourself into the scene as a participant or as an observer.

→ **Mystery of Faith:** Make comparisons and analogies ("the Kingdom of Heaven is like ...").

Observe *What main ideas or impressions stood out during meditation?*

Reflect *What seems significant about these observations for your life right now?*

Converse *How is God speaking to your heart through this meditation?*

Act *What practical step can you take to bring your meditation to life in your actions today?*

JOURNAL ENTRY

"Whoever perseveres in prayer shall be saved, and for those who do not persevere in prayer, there is no certainty of salvation."

ST. ALPHONSUS LIGUORI

EVENING EXAMEN

Examine your conscience about the thoughts, words, deeds, and omissions of this day. Then, with true repentance, pray an **Act of Contrition**: "O my God, I am heartily sorry for having offended Thee, and I detest all my sins because of Thy just punishments, but most of all because they offend Thee, my God, who art all good and deserving of all my love. I firmly resolve with the help of Thy grace to sin no more and to avoid the near occasion of sin. Amen."

Our Father. Hail Mary. Glory Be.

Session 43 | / / | Source: | Adoration? Y / N

GOD'S PRESENCE

"The Lord stood by me and gave me strength, so that through me the message might be fully proclaimed ..." – **2 Timothy 4:17**

Subject *Write or describe the **quotation, scene or event,** or **mystery** that you will meditate on.*

○ SPIRITUAL QUOTATION | ○ SCENE OR EVENT | ○ MYSTERY OF FAITH

MEDITATION

→ **Spiritual quotation:** Read and reread the quotation deliberately and meditatively.

→ **Scene or Event:** Attempt to place yourself into the scene as a participant or as an observer.

→ **Mystery of Faith:** Make comparisons and analogies ("the Kingdom of Heaven is like ...").

Observe *What main ideas or impressions stood out during meditation?*

Reflect *What seems significant about these observations for your life right now?*

Converse *How is God speaking to your heart through this meditation?*

Act *What practical step can you take to bring your meditation to life in your actions today?*

JOURNAL ENTRY

"To one who has faith, no explanation is necessary. To one without faith, no explanation is possible."

ST. THOMAS AQUINAS

EVENING EXAMEN

Examine your conscience about the thoughts, words, deeds, and omissions of this day. Then, with true repentance, pray an **Act of Contrition**: "O my God, I am heartily sorry for having offended Thee, and I detest all my sins because of Thy just punishments, but most of all because they offend Thee, my God, who art all good and deserving of all my love. I firmly resolve with the help of Thy grace to sin no more and to avoid the near occasion of sin. Amen."

Our Father. Hail Mary. Glory Be.

GOD'S PRESENCE

"The Lord is your keeper; the Lord is your shade at your right hand." – **Psalm 121:5**

Subject *Write or describe the* ***quotation, scene or event,*** *or* ***mystery*** *that you will meditate on.*

○ SPIRITUAL QUOTATION | ○ SCENE OR EVENT | ○ MYSTERY OF FAITH

MEDITATION

→ **Spiritual quotation:** Read and reread the quotation deliberately and meditatively.
→ **Scene or Event:** Attempt to place yourself into the scene as a participant or as an observer.
→ **Mystery of Faith:** Make comparisons and analogies ("the Kingdom of Heaven is like ...").

Observe *What main ideas or impressions stood out during meditation?*

Reflect *What seems significant about these observations for your life right now?*

Converse *How is God speaking to your heart through this meditation?*

Act *What practical step can you take to bring your meditation to life in your actions today?*

JOURNAL ENTRY

"Prayer is the raising of the mind to God. We must always remember this. The actual words matter less."

POPE ST. JOHN PAUL II

EVENING EXAMEN

Examine your conscience about the thoughts, words, deeds, and omissions of this day. Then, with true repentance, pray an **Act of Contrition**: "O my God, I am heartily sorry for having offended Thee, and I detest all my sins because of Thy just punishments, but most of all because they offend Thee, my God, who art all good and deserving of all my love. I firmly resolve with the help of Thy grace to sin no more and to avoid the near occasion of sin. Amen."

Our Father. Hail Mary. Glory Be.

Session 45 | / / | Source: | Adoration? Y / N

GOD'S PRESENCE

"... I know the plans I have for you ... plans for your welfare and not for harm, to give you a future with hope." – **Jeremiah 29:11**

Subject *Write or describe the **quotation, scene or event,** or **mystery** that you will meditate on.*

○ SPIRITUAL QUOTATION | ○ SCENE OR EVENT | ○ MYSTERY OF FAITH

MEDITATION

→ **Spiritual quotation:** Read and reread the quotation deliberately and meditatively.

→ **Scene or Event:** Attempt to place yourself into the scene as a participant or as an observer.

→ **Mystery of Faith:** Make comparisons and analogies ("the Kingdom of Heaven is like ...").

Observe *What main ideas or impressions stood out during meditation?*

Reflect *What seems significant about these observations for your life right now?*

Converse *How is God speaking to your heart through this meditation?*

Act *What practical step can you take to bring your meditation to life in your actions today?*

JOURNAL ENTRY

"If we wish to follow Christ closely, we cannot choose an easy, quiet life. It will be a demanding path, but one that brings much joy."

POPE BENEDICT XVI

EVENING EXAMEN

Examine your conscience about the thoughts, words, deeds, and omissions of this day. Then, with true repentance, pray an **Act of Contrition**: "O my God, I am heartily sorry for having offended Thee, and I detest all my sins because of Thy just punishments, but most of all because they offend Thee, my God, who art all good and deserving of all my love. I firmly resolve with the help of Thy grace to sin no more and to avoid the near occasion of sin. Amen."

Our Father. Hail Mary. Glory Be.

Session 46 | / / | Source: | Adoration? Y / N

GOD'S PRESENCE

"The angel of the Lord appeared to him and said to him, 'The Lord is with you, you mighty warrior.'" – **Judges 6:12**

Subject *Write or describe the* ***quotation, scene or event,*** *or* ***mystery*** *that you will meditate on.*

○ SPIRITUAL QUOTATION | ○ SCENE OR EVENT | ○ MYSTERY OF FAITH

MEDITATION

→ **Spiritual quotation:** Read and reread the quotation deliberately and meditatively.

→ **Scene or Event:** Attempt to place yourself into the scene as a participant or as an observer.

→ **Mystery of Faith:** Make comparisons and analogies ("the Kingdom of Heaven is like ...").

Observe *What main ideas or impressions stood out during meditation?*

Reflect *What seems significant about these observations for your life right now?*

Converse *How is God speaking to your heart through this meditation?*

Act *What practical step can you take to bring your meditation to life in your actions today?*

JOURNAL ENTRY

"Let us not be content to listen to the Word of God in silence, but let us meditate on it and put it into practice in our lives."

POPE FRANCIS

EVENING EXAMEN

Examine your conscience about the thoughts, words, deeds, and omissions of this day. Then, with true repentance, pray an **Act of Contrition**: "O my God, I am heartily sorry for having offended Thee, and I detest all my sins because of Thy just punishments, but most of all because they offend Thee, my God, who art all good and deserving of all my love. I firmly resolve with the help of Thy grace to sin no more and to avoid the near occasion of sin. Amen."

Our Father. Hail Mary. Glory Be.

Session 47 | / / | Source: | Adoration? Y / N

GOD'S PRESENCE

"I will instruct you and teach you the way you should go; I will counsel you with my eye upon you." **– Psalm 32:8**

Subject *Write or describe the* ***quotation, scene or event,*** *or* ***mystery*** *that you will meditate on.*

○ SPIRITUAL QUOTATION | ○ SCENE OR EVENT | ○ MYSTERY OF FAITH

MEDITATION

→ **Spiritual quotation:** Read and reread the quotation deliberately and meditatively.

→ **Scene or Event:** Attempt to place yourself into the scene as a participant or as an observer.

→ **Mystery of Faith:** Make comparisons and analogies ("the Kingdom of Heaven is like ...").

Observe *What main ideas or impressions stood out during meditation?*

Reflect *What seems significant about these observations for your life right now?*

Converse *How is God speaking to your heart through this meditation?*

Act *What practical step can you take to bring your meditation to life in your actions today?*

JOURNAL ENTRY

"One day of humble prayer will not only bring more grace, but will do more for the Church than many days of activism."

ST. TERESA OF ÁVILA

EVENING EXAMEN

Examine your conscience about the thoughts, words, deeds, and omissions of this day. Then, with true repentance, pray an **Act of Contrition**: "O my God, I am heartily sorry for having offended Thee, and I detest all my sins because of Thy just punishments, but most of all because they offend Thee, my God, who art all good and deserving of all my love. I firmly resolve with the help of Thy grace to sin no more and to avoid the near occasion of sin. Amen."

Our Father. Hail Mary. Glory Be.

Session 48 | / / | Source: | Adoration? Y / N

GOD'S PRESENCE

"I can do all things through him who strengthens me." – **Philippians 4:13**

Subject *Write or describe the **quotation, scene or event,** or **mystery** that you will meditate on.*

○ SPIRITUAL QUOTATION | ○ SCENE OR EVENT | ○ MYSTERY OF FAITH

MEDITATION

→ **Spiritual quotation:** Read and reread the quotation deliberately and meditatively.

→ **Scene or Event:** Attempt to place yourself into the scene as a participant or as an observer.

→ **Mystery of Faith:** Make comparisons and analogies ("the Kingdom of Heaven is like ...").

Observe *What main ideas or impressions stood out during meditation?*

Reflect *What seems significant about these observations for your life right now?*

Converse *How is God speaking to your heart through this meditation?*

Act *What practical step can you take to bring your meditation to life in your actions today?*

JOURNAL ENTRY

"Faith and prayer are the wings of the soul. When one fails, the soul falls to the earth; with both, the soul ascends to God."

ST. JOHN OF THE CROSS

EVENING EXAMEN

Examine your conscience about the thoughts, words, deeds, and omissions of this day. Then, with true repentance, pray an **Act of Contrition**: "O my God, I am heartily sorry for having offended Thee, and I detest all my sins because of Thy just punishments, but most of all because they offend Thee, my God, who art all good and deserving of all my love. I firmly resolve with the help of Thy grace to sin no more and to avoid the near occasion of sin. Amen."

Our Father. Hail Mary. Glory Be.

GOD'S PRESENCE

"And he said, 'My presence will go with you, and I will give you rest.'" – **Exodus 33:14**

Subject *Write or describe the **quotation, scene or event,** or **mystery** that you will meditate on.*

○ SPIRITUAL QUOTATION | ○ SCENE OR EVENT | ○ MYSTERY OF FAITH

MEDITATION

→ **Spiritual quotation:** Read and reread the quotation deliberately and meditatively.

→ **Scene or Event:** Attempt to place yourself into the scene as a participant or as an observer.

→ **Mystery of Faith:** Make comparisons and analogies ("the Kingdom of Heaven is like ...").

Observe *What main ideas or impressions stood out during meditation?*

Reflect *What seems significant about these observations for your life right now?*

Converse *How is God speaking to your heart through this meditation?*

Act *What practical step can you take to bring your meditation to life in your actions today?*

JOURNAL ENTRY

"Do not be discouraged by the difficulty of prayer. It is in the struggle that God draws us closer to Himself."

ST. PIO OF PIETRELCINA (PADRE PIO)

EVENING EXAMEN

Examine your conscience about the thoughts, words, deeds, and omissions of this day. Then, with true repentance, pray an **Act of Contrition**: "O my God, I am heartily sorry for having offended Thee, and I detest all my sins because of Thy just punishments, but most of all because they offend Thee, my God, who art all good and deserving of all my love. I firmly resolve with the help of Thy grace to sin no more and to avoid the near occasion of sin. Amen."

Our Father. Hail Mary. Glory Be.

Session 50 | / / | Source: | Adoration? Y / N

GOD'S PRESENCE

"But the Lord is faithful; he will strengthen you and guard you from the evil one." – **2 Thessalonians 3:3**

Subject *Write or describe the **quotation, scene or event,** or **mystery** that you will meditate on.*

○ SPIRITUAL QUOTATION | ○ SCENE OR EVENT | ○ MYSTERY OF FAITH

MEDITATION

→ **Spiritual quotation:** Read and reread the quotation deliberately and meditatively.

→ **Scene or Event:** Attempt to place yourself into the scene as a participant or as an observer.

→ **Mystery of Faith:** Make comparisons and analogies ("the Kingdom of Heaven is like ...").

Observe *What main ideas or impressions stood out during meditation?*

Reflect *What seems significant about these observations for your life right now?*

Converse *How is God speaking to your heart through this meditation?*

Act *What practical step can you take to bring your meditation to life in your actions today?*

JOURNAL ENTRY

"We need to find God, and He cannot be found in noise and restlessness. God is the friend of silence."

ST. TERESA OF CALCUTTA

EVENING EXAMEN

Examine your conscience about the thoughts, words, deeds, and omissions of this day. Then, with true repentance, pray an **Act of Contrition**: "O my God, I am heartily sorry for having offended Thee, and I detest all my sins because of Thy just punishments, but most of all because they offend Thee, my God, who art all good and deserving of all my love. I firmly resolve with the help of Thy grace to sin no more and to avoid the near occasion of sin. Amen."

Our Father. Hail Mary. Glory Be.

Session 51 | / / | Source: | Adoration? Y / N

GOD'S PRESENCE

"For we walk by faith, not by sight." **– 2 Corinthians 5:7**

Subject *Write or describe the* ***quotation, scene or event,*** *or* ***mystery*** *that you will meditate on.*

○ SPIRITUAL QUOTATION | ○ SCENE OR EVENT | ○ MYSTERY OF FAITH

MEDITATION

→ **Spiritual quotation:** Read and reread the quotation deliberately and meditatively.

→ **Scene or Event:** Attempt to place yourself into the scene as a participant or as an observer.

→ **Mystery of Faith:** Make comparisons and analogies ("the Kingdom of Heaven is like ...").

Observe *What main ideas or impressions stood out during meditation?*

Reflect *What seems significant about these observations for your life right now?*

Converse *How is God speaking to your heart through this meditation?*

Act *What practical step can you take to bring your meditation to life in your actions today?*

JOURNAL ENTRY

"In the face of trials and difficulties, prayer is our refuge, for in it we find God's strength and peace."

ST. JOHN PAUL II

EVENING EXAMEN

Examine your conscience about the thoughts, words, deeds, and omissions of this day. Then, with true repentance, pray an **Act of Contrition**: "O my God, I am heartily sorry for having offended Thee, and I detest all my sins because of Thy just punishments, but most of all because they offend Thee, my God, who art all good and deserving of all my love. I firmly resolve with the help of Thy grace to sin no more and to avoid the near occasion of sin. Amen."

Our Father. Hail Mary. Glory Be.

GOD'S PRESENCE

"The eyes of the Lord are on the righteous, and his ears are open to their cry." – **Psalm 34:15**

Subject *Write or describe the **quotation, scene or event,** or **mystery** that you will meditate on.*

○ SPIRITUAL QUOTATION | ○ SCENE OR EVENT | ○ MYSTERY OF FAITH

MEDITATION

→ **Spiritual quotation:** Read and reread the quotation deliberately and meditatively.

→ **Scene or Event:** Attempt to place yourself into the scene as a participant or as an observer.

→ **Mystery of Faith:** Make comparisons and analogies ("the Kingdom of Heaven is like ...").

Observe *What main ideas or impressions stood out during meditation?*

Reflect *What seems significant about these observations for your life right now?*

Converse *How is God speaking to your heart through this meditation?*

Act *What practical step can you take to bring your meditation to life in your actions today?*

JOURNAL ENTRY

"Prayer, fasting, and works of mercy are the best means of helping us advance in holiness."

POPE LEO XIII

EVENING EXAMEN

Examine your conscience about the thoughts, words, deeds, and omissions of this day. Then, with true repentance, pray an **Act of Contrition**: "O my God, I am heartily sorry for having offended Thee, and I detest all my sins because of Thy just punishments, but most of all because they offend Thee, my God, who art all good and deserving of all my love. I firmly resolve with the help of Thy grace to sin no more and to avoid the near occasion of sin. Amen."

Our Father. Hail Mary. Glory Be.

Session 53 | / / | Source: | Adoration? Y / N

GOD'S PRESENCE

"The Lord is good to all, and his compassion is over all that he has made." – **Psalm 145:9**

Subject *Write or describe the **quotation, scene or event,** or **mystery** that you will meditate on.*

○ SPIRITUAL QUOTATION | ○ SCENE OR EVENT | ○ MYSTERY OF FAITH

MEDITATION

→ **Spiritual quotation:** Read and reread the quotation deliberately and meditatively.

→ **Scene or Event:** Attempt to place yourself into the scene as a participant or as an observer.

→ **Mystery of Faith:** Make comparisons and analogies ("the Kingdom of Heaven is like …").

Observe *What main ideas or impressions stood out during meditation?*

Reflect *What seems significant about these observations for your life right now?*

Converse *How is God speaking to your heart through this meditation?*

Act *What practical step can you take to bring your meditation to life in your actions today?*

JOURNAL ENTRY

"Prayer is the breath of the soul; without it, we wither and die. It is our connection to the life-giving power of God's grace."

ST. AUGUSTINE OF HIPPO

EVENING EXAMEN

Examine your conscience about the thoughts, words, deeds, and omissions of this day. Then, with true repentance, pray an **Act of Contrition**: "O my God, I am heartily sorry for having offended Thee, and I detest all my sins because of Thy just punishments, but most of all because they offend Thee, my God, who art all good and deserving of all my love. I firmly resolve with the help of Thy grace to sin no more and to avoid the near occasion of sin. Amen."

Our Father. Hail Mary. Glory Be.

GOD'S PRESENCE

"For the mountains may depart and the hills be removed, but my steadfast love shall not depart from you ..." – **Isaiah 54:10**

Subject *Write or describe the **quotation, scene or event,** or **mystery** that you will meditate on.*

○ SPIRITUAL QUOTATION | ○ SCENE OR EVENT | ○ MYSTERY OF FAITH

MEDITATION

→ **Spiritual quotation:** Read and reread the quotation deliberately and meditatively.

→ **Scene or Event:** Attempt to place yourself into the scene as a participant or as an observer.

→ **Mystery of Faith:** Make comparisons and analogies ("the Kingdom of Heaven is like ...").

Observe *What main ideas or impressions stood out during meditation?*

Reflect *What seems significant about these observations for your life right now?*

Converse *How is God speaking to your heart through this meditation?*

Act *What practical step can you take to bring your meditation to life in your actions today?*

JOURNAL ENTRY

"By turning our minds and hearts to God in meditation, we open ourselves to the transforming power of His grace."

ST. GREGORY THE GREAT

EVENING EXAMEN

Examine your conscience about the thoughts, words, deeds, and omissions of this day. Then, with true repentance, pray an **Act of Contrition**: "O my God, I am heartily sorry for having offended Thee, and I detest all my sins because of Thy just punishments, but most of all because they offend Thee, my God, who art all good and deserving of all my love. I firmly resolve with the help of Thy grace to sin no more and to avoid the near occasion of sin. Amen."

Our Father. Hail Mary. Glory Be.

Session 55 | / / | Source: | Adoration? Y / N

GOD'S PRESENCE

"Strive first for the kingdom of God and his righteousness, and all these things will be given to you as well." – **Matthew 6:33**

Subject *Write or describe the* ***quotation, scene or event,*** *or* ***mystery*** *that you will meditate on.*

○ SPIRITUAL QUOTATION | ○ SCENE OR EVENT | ○ MYSTERY OF FAITH

MEDITATION

→ **Spiritual quotation:** Read and reread the quotation deliberately and meditatively.

→ **Scene or Event:** Attempt to place yourself into the scene as a participant or as an observer.

→ **Mystery of Faith:** Make comparisons and analogies ("the Kingdom of Heaven is like ...").

Observe *What main ideas or impressions stood out during meditation?*

Reflect *What seems significant about these observations for your life right now?*

Converse *How is God speaking to your heart through this meditation?*

Act *What practical step can you take to bring your meditation to life in your actions today?*

JOURNAL ENTRY

"Through meditation, we lift our minds above the distractions of this world, to contemplate the eternal truths of God."

ST. JOHN HENRY NEWMAN

EVENING EXAMEN

Examine your conscience about the thoughts, words, deeds, and omissions of this day. Then, with true repentance, pray an **Act of Contrition**: "O my God, I am heartily sorry for having offended Thee, and I detest all my sins because of Thy just punishments, but most of all because they offend Thee, my God, who art all good and deserving of all my love. I firmly resolve with the help of Thy grace to sin no more and to avoid the near occasion of sin. Amen."

Our Father. Hail Mary. Glory Be.

Session 56 | / / | Source: | Adoration? Y / N

GOD'S PRESENCE

"Where can I go from your spirit? Or where can I flee from your presence?" – **Psalm 139:7**

Subject *Write or describe the **quotation, scene or event,** or **mystery** that you will meditate on.*

○ SPIRITUAL QUOTATION | ○ SCENE OR EVENT | ○ MYSTERY OF FAITH

MEDITATION

→ **Spiritual quotation:** Read and reread the quotation deliberately and meditatively.

→ **Scene or Event:** Attempt to place yourself into the scene as a participant or as an observer.

→ **Mystery of Faith:** Make comparisons and analogies ("the Kingdom of Heaven is like ...").

Observe *What main ideas or impressions stood out during meditation?*

Reflect *What seems significant about these observations for your life right now?*

Converse *How is God speaking to your heart through this meditation?*

Act *What practical step can you take to bring your meditation to life in your actions today?*

JOURNAL ENTRY

"In prayer, God reveals the desires of our hearts and aligns them with His holy will."

ST. BERNARD OF CLAIRVAUX

EVENING EXAMEN

Examine your conscience about the thoughts, words, deeds, and omissions of this day. Then, with true repentance, pray an **Act of Contrition**: "O my God, I am heartily sorry for having offended Thee, and I detest all my sins because of Thy just punishments, but most of all because they offend Thee, my God, who art all good and deserving of all my love. I firmly resolve with the help of Thy grace to sin no more and to avoid the near occasion of sin. Amen."

Our Father. Hail Mary. Glory Be.

Session 57 | / / | Source: | Adoration? Y / N

GOD'S PRESENCE

"All who obey his commandments abide in him, and he abides in them." **– 1 John 3:24**

Subject *Write or describe the **quotation, scene or event,** or **mystery** that you will meditate on.*

○ SPIRITUAL QUOTATION | ○ SCENE OR EVENT | ○ MYSTERY OF FAITH

MEDITATION

→ **Spiritual quotation:** Read and reread the quotation deliberately and meditatively.

→ **Scene or Event:** Attempt to place yourself into the scene as a participant or as an observer.

→ **Mystery of Faith:** Make comparisons and analogies ("the Kingdom of Heaven is like ...").

Observe *What main ideas or impressions stood out during meditation?*

Reflect *What seems significant about these observations for your life right now?*

Converse *How is God speaking to your heart through this meditation?*

Act *What practical step can you take to bring your meditation to life in your actions today?*

JOURNAL ENTRY

"Prayer is the strength of the soul, and the virtue which raises it to heaven."

ST. JOHN CHRYSOSTOM

EVENING EXAMEN

Examine your conscience about the thoughts, words, deeds, and omissions of this day. Then, with true repentance, pray an **Act of Contrition**: "O my God, I am heartily sorry for having offended Thee, and I detest all my sins because of Thy just punishments, but most of all because they offend Thee, my God, who art all good and deserving of all my love. I firmly resolve with the help of Thy grace to sin no more and to avoid the near occasion of sin. Amen."

Our Father. Hail Mary. Glory Be.

Session 58 | / / | Source: | Adoration? Y / N

GOD'S PRESENCE

"The one who calls you is faithful, and he will do this." **– 1 Thessalonians 5:24**

Subject *Write or describe the **quotation, scene or event,** or **mystery** that you will meditate on.*

○ SPIRITUAL QUOTATION | ○ SCENE OR EVENT | ○ MYSTERY OF FAITH

MEDITATION

→ **Spiritual quotation:** Read and reread the quotation deliberately and meditatively.

→ **Scene or Event:** Attempt to place yourself into the scene as a participant or as an observer.

→ **Mystery of Faith:** Make comparisons and analogies ("the Kingdom of Heaven is like ...").

Observe *What main ideas or impressions stood out during meditation?*

Reflect *What seems significant about these observations for your life right now?*

Converse *How is God speaking to your heart through this meditation?*

Act *What practical step can you take to bring your meditation to life in your actions today?*

JOURNAL ENTRY

"Pray for the grace of self-knowledge and the ability to discern God's will, for therein lies the peace of your soul."

ST. IGNATIUS OF LOYOLA

EVENING EXAMEN

Examine your conscience about the thoughts, words, deeds, and omissions of this day. Then, with true repentance, pray an **Act of Contrition**: "O my God, I am heartily sorry for having offended Thee, and I detest all my sins because of Thy just punishments, but most of all because they offend Thee, my God, who art all good and deserving of all my love. I firmly resolve with the help of Thy grace to sin no more and to avoid the near occasion of sin. Amen."

Our Father. Hail Mary. Glory Be.

GOD'S PRESENCE

"And I will ask the Father, and he will give you another Advocate, to be with you forever." – **John 14:16**

Subject *Write or describe the **quotation, scene or event,** or **mystery** that you will meditate on.*

○ SPIRITUAL QUOTATION | ○ SCENE OR EVENT | ○ MYSTERY OF FAITH

MEDITATION

→ **Spiritual quotation:** Read and reread the quotation deliberately and meditatively.
→ **Scene or Event:** Attempt to place yourself into the scene as a participant or as an observer.
→ **Mystery of Faith:** Make comparisons and analogies ("the Kingdom of Heaven is like ...").

Observe *What main ideas or impressions stood out during meditation?*

Reflect *What seems significant about these observations for your life right now?*

Converse *How is God speaking to your heart through this meditation?*

Act *What practical step can you take to bring your meditation to life in your actions today?*

JOURNAL ENTRY

"Meditation is the key to growth in faith; through it, we grow in understanding of God's will and His love for us."

ST. BASIL THE GREAT

EVENING EXAMEN

Examine your conscience about the thoughts, words, deeds, and omissions of this day. Then, with true repentance, pray an **Act of Contrition**: "O my God, I am heartily sorry for having offended Thee, and I detest all my sins because of Thy just punishments, but most of all because they offend Thee, my God, who art all good and deserving of all my love. I firmly resolve with the help of Thy grace to sin no more and to avoid the near occasion of sin. Amen."

Our Father. Hail Mary. Glory Be.

GOD'S PRESENCE

"Yet you are near, O Lord, and all your commandments are true." – **Psalm 119:151**

Subject *Write or describe the **quotation, scene or event,** or **mystery** that you will meditate on.*

○ SPIRITUAL QUOTATION | ○ SCENE OR EVENT | ○ MYSTERY OF FAITH

MEDITATION

→ **Spiritual quotation:** Read and reread the quotation deliberately and meditatively.

→ **Scene or Event:** Attempt to place yourself into the scene as a participant or as an observer.

→ **Mystery of Faith:** Make comparisons and analogies ("the Kingdom of Heaven is like ...").

Observe *What main ideas or impressions stood out during meditation?*

Reflect *What seems significant about these observations for your life right now?*

Converse *How is God speaking to your heart through this meditation?*

Act *What practical step can you take to bring your meditation to life in your actions today?*

JOURNAL ENTRY

"The more you devote yourself in prayer, the more you will sense God's closeness and be filled with His peace."

ST. FAUSTINA KOWALSKA

EVENING EXAMEN

Examine your conscience about the thoughts, words, deeds, and omissions of this day. Then, with true repentance, pray an **Act of Contrition**: "O my God, I am heartily sorry for having offended Thee, and I detest all my sins because of Thy just punishments, but most of all because they offend Thee, my God, who art all good and deserving of all my love. I firmly resolve with the help of Thy grace to sin no more and to avoid the near occasion of sin. Amen."

Our Father. Hail Mary. Glory Be.

MONTH 3

TRANSFORMATION THROUGH PRAYER

As you enter this final month, consider how far you've come and how God is transforming your soul. Prayer is a lifelong journey and these shifts and changes are only the beginning. Reflect on the transformation happening within your heart.

What transformation have you noticed in your sense of peace or God's presence?

How has meditation helped you to better discern God's will for your life?

What struggles in prayer have you overcome, and what still remains?

In what ways are you seeing the fruits of prayer in your relationships and actions?

How do you plan to continue the journey after this journal is complete?

Session 61 | / / | Source: | Adoration? Y / N

GOD'S PRESENCE

"The Lord is my strength and my might, and he has become my salvation ..." – **Exodus 15:2**

Subject *Write or describe the **quotation, scene or event,** or **mystery** that you will meditate on.*

○ SPIRITUAL QUOTATION | ○ SCENE OR EVENT | ○ MYSTERY OF FAITH

MEDITATION

→ **Spiritual quotation:** Read and reread the quotation deliberately and meditatively.

→ **Scene or Event:** Attempt to place yourself into the scene as a participant or as an observer.

→ **Mystery of Faith:** Make comparisons and analogies ("the Kingdom of Heaven is like ...").

Observe *What main ideas or impressions stood out during meditation?*

Reflect *What seems significant about these observations for your life right now?*

Converse *How is God speaking to your heart through this meditation?*

Act *What practical step can you take to bring your meditation to life in your actions today?*

JOURNAL ENTRY

"Let your daily prayer be a constant offering to God, so that every moment of your life is a dialogue with Him."

POPE PAUL VI

EVENING EXAMEN

Examine your conscience about the thoughts, words, deeds, and omissions of this day. Then, with true repentance, pray an **Act of Contrition**: "O my God, I am heartily sorry for having offended Thee, and I detest all my sins because of Thy just punishments, but most of all because they offend Thee, my God, who art all good and deserving of all my love. I firmly resolve with the help of Thy grace to sin no more and to avoid the near occasion of sin. Amen."

Our Father. Hail Mary. Glory Be.

Session 62 | / / | Source: | Adoration? Y / N

GOD'S PRESENCE

"God is love, and those who abide in love abide in God ..." **– 1 John 4:16**

Subject *Write or describe the* ***quotation, scene or event,*** *or* ***mystery*** *that you will meditate on.*

○ SPIRITUAL QUOTATION | ○ SCENE OR EVENT | ○ MYSTERY OF FAITH

MEDITATION

→ **Spiritual quotation:** Read and reread the quotation deliberately and meditatively.

→ **Scene or Event:** Attempt to place yourself into the scene as a participant or as an observer.

→ **Mystery of Faith:** Make comparisons and analogies ("the Kingdom of Heaven is like ...").

Observe *What main ideas or impressions stood out during meditation?*

Reflect *What seems significant about these observations for your life right now?*

Converse *How is God speaking to your heart through this meditation?*

Act *What practical step can you take to bring your meditation to life in your actions today?*

JOURNAL ENTRY

"Rejoice in hope, be patient in tribulation, be constant in prayer."

ROMANS 12:12

EVENING EXAMEN

Examine your conscience about the thoughts, words, deeds, and omissions of this day. Then, with true repentance, pray an **Act of Contrition**: "O my God, I am heartily sorry for having offended Thee, and I detest all my sins because of Thy just punishments, but most of all because they offend Thee, my God, who art all good and deserving of all my love. I firmly resolve with the help of Thy grace to sin no more and to avoid the near occasion of sin. Amen."

Our Father. Hail Mary. Glory Be.

GOD'S PRESENCE

"Trust in the Lord with all your heart, and do not rely on your own insight." – **Proverbs 3:5**

Subject *Write or describe the* ***quotation, scene or event,*** *or* ***mystery*** *that you will meditate on.*

○ SPIRITUAL QUOTATION | ○ SCENE OR EVENT | ○ MYSTERY OF FAITH

MEDITATION

→ **Spiritual quotation:** Read and reread the quotation deliberately and meditatively.

→ **Scene or Event:** Attempt to place yourself into the scene as a participant or as an observer.

→ **Mystery of Faith:** Make comparisons and analogies ("the Kingdom of Heaven is like ...").

Observe *What main ideas or impressions stood out during meditation?*

Reflect *What seems significant about these observations for your life right now?*

Converse *How is God speaking to your heart through this meditation?*

Act *What practical step can you take to bring your meditation to life in your actions today?*

JOURNAL ENTRY

"Pray without ceasing, give thanks in all circumstances; for this is the will of God in Christ Jesus for you."

1 THESSALONIANS 5:17-18

EVENING EXAMEN

Examine your conscience about the thoughts, words, deeds, and omissions of this day. Then, with true repentance, pray an **Act of Contrition**: "O my God, I am heartily sorry for having offended Thee, and I detest all my sins because of Thy just punishments, but most of all because they offend Thee, my God, who art all good and deserving of all my love. I firmly resolve with the help of Thy grace to sin no more and to avoid the near occasion of sin. Amen."

Our Father. Hail Mary. Glory Be.

Session 64 | / / | Source: | Adoration? Y / N

GOD'S PRESENCE

"The Lord is my rock, my fortress, and my deliverer, my God, my rock in whom I take refuge ..." – **Psalm 18:2**

Subject *Write or describe the **quotation, scene or event,** or **mystery** that you will meditate on.*

○ SPIRITUAL QUOTATION | ○ SCENE OR EVENT | ○ MYSTERY OF FAITH

MEDITATION

→ **Spiritual quotation:** Read and reread the quotation deliberately and meditatively.

→ **Scene or Event:** Attempt to place yourself into the scene as a participant or as an observer.

→ **Mystery of Faith:** Make comparisons and analogies ("the Kingdom of Heaven is like ...").

Observe *What main ideas or impressions stood out during meditation?*

Reflect *What seems significant about these observations for your life right now?*

Converse *How is God speaking to your heart through this meditation?*

Act *What practical step can you take to bring your meditation to life in your actions today?*

JOURNAL ENTRY

"I love the Lord, because he has heard my voice and my supplications."

PSALM 116:1

EVENING EXAMEN

Examine your conscience about the thoughts, words, deeds, and omissions of this day. Then, with true repentance, pray an **Act of Contrition**: "O my God, I am heartily sorry for having offended Thee, and I detest all my sins because of Thy just punishments, but most of all because they offend Thee, my God, who art all good and deserving of all my love. I firmly resolve with the help of Thy grace to sin no more and to avoid the near occasion of sin. Amen."

Our Father. Hail Mary. Glory Be.

Session 65 | / / | Source: | Adoration? Y / N

GOD'S PRESENCE

"The Lord is a stronghold for the oppressed, a stronghold in times of trouble." – **Psalm 9:9**

Subject *Write or describe the **quotation, scene or event,** or **mystery** that you will meditate on.*

○ SPIRITUAL QUOTATION | ○ SCENE OR EVENT | ○ MYSTERY OF FAITH

MEDITATION

→ **Spiritual quotation:** Read and reread the quotation deliberately and meditatively.

→ **Scene or Event:** Attempt to place yourself into the scene as a participant or as an observer.

→ **Mystery of Faith:** Make comparisons and analogies ("the Kingdom of Heaven is like ...").

Observe *What main ideas or impressions stood out during meditation?*

Reflect *What seems significant about these observations for your life right now?*

Converse *How is God speaking to your heart through this meditation?*

Act *What practical step can you take to bring your meditation to life in your actions today?*

JOURNAL ENTRY

"Do not be anxious about anything, but in everything by prayer and supplication with thanksgiving let your requests be made known to God."

PHILIPPIANS 4:6

EVENING EXAMEN

Examine your conscience about the thoughts, words, deeds, and omissions of this day. Then, with true repentance, pray an **Act of Contrition**: "O my God, I am heartily sorry for having offended Thee, and I detest all my sins because of Thy just punishments, but most of all because they offend Thee, my God, who art all good and deserving of all my love. I firmly resolve with the help of Thy grace to sin no more and to avoid the near occasion of sin. Amen."

Our Father. Hail Mary. Glory Be.

Session 66 | / / | Source: | Adoration? Y / N

GOD'S PRESENCE

"When you go out to war ... do not be afraid of [your enemies], for the Lord your God is with you ..." – **Deuteronomy 20:1**

Subject *Write or describe the **quotation, scene or event,** or **mystery** that you will meditate on.*

○ SPIRITUAL QUOTATION | ○ SCENE OR EVENT | ○ MYSTERY OF FAITH

MEDITATION

→ **Spiritual quotation:** Read and reread the quotation deliberately and meditatively.

→ **Scene or Event:** Attempt to place yourself into the scene as a participant or as an observer.

→ **Mystery of Faith:** Make comparisons and analogies ("the Kingdom of Heaven is like ...").

Observe *What main ideas or impressions stood out during meditation?*

Reflect *What seems significant about these observations for your life right now?*

Converse *How is God speaking to your heart through this meditation?*

Act *What practical step can you take to bring your meditation to life in your actions today?*

JOURNAL ENTRY

"The Lord is far from the wicked, but he hears the prayer of the righteous."

PROVERBS 15:29

EVENING EXAMEN

Examine your conscience about the thoughts, words, deeds, and omissions of this day. Then, with true repentance, pray an **Act of Contrition**: "O my God, I am heartily sorry for having offended Thee, and I detest all my sins because of Thy just punishments, but most of all because they offend Thee, my God, who art all good and deserving of all my love. I firmly resolve with the help of Thy grace to sin no more and to avoid the near occasion of sin. Amen."

Our Father. Hail Mary. Glory Be.

Session 67 | / / | Source: | Adoration? Y / N

GOD'S PRESENCE

"When I am afraid, I put my trust in you." – **Psalm 56:3**

Subject *Write or describe the **quotation, scene or event,** or **mystery** that you will meditate on.*

○ SPIRITUAL QUOTATION | ○ SCENE OR EVENT | ○ MYSTERY OF FAITH

MEDITATION

→ **Spiritual quotation:** Read and reread the quotation deliberately and meditatively.

→ **Scene or Event:** Attempt to place yourself into the scene as a participant or as an observer.

→ **Mystery of Faith:** Make comparisons and analogies ("the Kingdom of Heaven is like ...").

Observe *What main ideas or impressions stood out during meditation?*

Reflect *What seems significant about these observations for your life right now?*

Converse *How is God speaking to your heart through this meditation?*

Act *What practical step can you take to bring your meditation to life in your actions today?*

JOURNAL ENTRY

"The greater your trust in God, the more He will do for you."

ST. TERESA OF ÁVILA

EVENING EXAMEN

Examine your conscience about the thoughts, words, deeds, and omissions of this day. Then, with true repentance, pray an **Act of Contrition**: "O my God, I am heartily sorry for having offended Thee, and I detest all my sins because of Thy just punishments, but most of all because they offend Thee, my God, who art all good and deserving of all my love. I firmly resolve with the help of Thy grace to sin no more and to avoid the near occasion of sin. Amen."

Our Father. Hail Mary. Glory Be.

GOD'S PRESENCE

"Sing and rejoice, O daughter Zion! For lo, I will come and dwell in your midst, says the Lord." – **Zechariah 2:10**

Subject *Write or describe the* ***quotation, scene or event,*** *or* ***mystery*** *that you will meditate on.*

○ SPIRITUAL QUOTATION | ○ SCENE OR EVENT | ○ MYSTERY OF FAITH

MEDITATION

→ **Spiritual quotation:** Read and reread the quotation deliberately and meditatively.

→ **Scene or Event:** Attempt to place yourself into the scene as a participant or as an observer.

→ **Mystery of Faith:** Make comparisons and analogies ("the Kingdom of Heaven is like ...").

Observe *What main ideas or impressions stood out during meditation?*

Reflect *What seems significant about these observations for your life right now?*

Converse *How is God speaking to your heart through this meditation?*

Act *What practical step can you take to bring your meditation to life in your actions today?*

JOURNAL ENTRY

"Prayer is powerful beyond limits when we turn to the Immaculata who is queen even of God's heart."

ST. MAXIMILIAN KOLBE

EVENING EXAMEN

Examine your conscience about the thoughts, words, deeds, and omissions of this day. Then, with true repentance, pray an **Act of Contrition**: "O my God, I am heartily sorry for having offended Thee, and I detest all my sins because of Thy just punishments, but most of all because they offend Thee, my God, who art all good and deserving of all my love. I firmly resolve with the help of Thy grace to sin no more and to avoid the near occasion of sin. Amen."

Our Father. Hail Mary. Glory Be.

Session 69 | / / | Source: | Adoration? Y / N

GOD'S PRESENCE

"In all your ways acknowledge him, and he will make straight your paths." – **Proverbs 3:6**

Subject *Write or describe the* ***quotation, scene or event,*** *or* ***mystery*** *that you will meditate on.*

○ SPIRITUAL QUOTATION | ○ SCENE OR EVENT | ○ MYSTERY OF FAITH

MEDITATION

→ **Spiritual quotation:** Read and reread the quotation deliberately and meditatively.

→ **Scene or Event:** Attempt to place yourself into the scene as a participant or as an observer.

→ **Mystery of Faith:** Make comparisons and analogies ("the Kingdom of Heaven is like ...").

Observe *What main ideas or impressions stood out during meditation?*

Reflect *What seems significant about these observations for your life right now?*

Converse *How is God speaking to your heart through this meditation?*

Act *What practical step can you take to bring your meditation to life in your actions today?*

JOURNAL ENTRY

"In silence, we leave the world in order to stand in the presence of God. The act of leaving behind noise is the beginning of a soul's transformation."

CARDINAL ROBERT SARAH

EVENING EXAMEN

Examine your conscience about the thoughts, words, deeds, and omissions of this day. Then, with true repentance, pray an **Act of Contrition**: "O my God, I am heartily sorry for having offended Thee, and I detest all my sins because of Thy just punishments, but most of all because they offend Thee, my God, who art all good and deserving of all my love. I firmly resolve with the help of Thy grace to sin no more and to avoid the near occasion of sin. Amen."

Our Father. Hail Mary. Glory Be.

Session 70 | / / | Source: | Adoration? Y / N

GOD'S PRESENCE

"In the shelter of your presence you hide them from human plots; you hold them safe under your shelter ..." – **Psalm 31:20**

Subject *Write or describe the* ***quotation, scene or event,*** *or* ***mystery*** *that you will meditate on.*

○ SPIRITUAL QUOTATION | ○ SCENE OR EVENT | ○ MYSTERY OF FAITH

MEDITATION

→ **Spiritual quotation:** Read and reread the quotation deliberately and meditatively.

→ **Scene or Event:** Attempt to place yourself into the scene as a participant or as an observer.

→ **Mystery of Faith:** Make comparisons and analogies ("the Kingdom of Heaven is like ...").

Observe *What main ideas or impressions stood out during meditation?*

Reflect *What seems significant about these observations for your life right now?*

Converse *How is God speaking to your heart through this meditation?*

Act *What practical step can you take to bring your meditation to life in your actions today?*

JOURNAL ENTRY

"You cannot attain to charity except through humility. You cannot attain to humility without God's grace."

ST. BERNARD OF CLAIRVAUX

EVENING EXAMEN

Examine your conscience about the thoughts, words, deeds, and omissions of this day. Then, with true repentance, pray an **Act of Contrition**: "O my God, I am heartily sorry for having offended Thee, and I detest all my sins because of Thy just punishments, but most of all because they offend Thee, my God, who art all good and deserving of all my love. I firmly resolve with the help of Thy grace to sin no more and to avoid the near occasion of sin. Amen."

Our Father. Hail Mary. Glory Be.

Session 71 | / / | Source: | Adoration? Y / N

GOD'S PRESENCE

"Those of steadfast mind you keep in peace—in peace because they trust in you." – **Isaiah 26:3**

Subject *Write or describe the* ***quotation, scene or event,*** *or* ***mystery*** *that you will meditate on.*

○ SPIRITUAL QUOTATION | ○ SCENE OR EVENT | ○ MYSTERY OF FAITH

MEDITATION

→ **Spiritual quotation:** Read and reread the quotation deliberately and meditatively.

→ **Scene or Event:** Attempt to place yourself into the scene as a participant or as an observer.

→ **Mystery of Faith:** Make comparisons and analogies ("the Kingdom of Heaven is like ...").

Observe *What main ideas or impressions stood out during meditation?*

Reflect *What seems significant about these observations for your life right now?*

Converse *How is God speaking to your heart through this meditation?*

Act *What practical step can you take to bring your meditation to life in your actions today?*

JOURNAL ENTRY

"God speaks silently, God speaks in your heart; if your heart is noisy, chattering, you will not hear."

ST. TERESA OF ÁVILA

EVENING EXAMEN

Examine your conscience about the thoughts, words, deeds, and omissions of this day. Then, with true repentance, pray an **Act of Contrition**: "O my God, I am heartily sorry for having offended Thee, and I detest all my sins because of Thy just punishments, but most of all because they offend Thee, my God, who art all good and deserving of all my love. I firmly resolve with the help of Thy grace to sin no more and to avoid the near occasion of sin. Amen."

Our Father. Hail Mary. Glory Be.

GOD'S PRESENCE

"Even there your hand shall lead me, and your right hand shall hold me fast." – **Psalm 139:10**

Subject *Write or describe the **quotation, scene or event,** or **mystery** that you will meditate on.*

○ SPIRITUAL QUOTATION | ○ SCENE OR EVENT | ○ MYSTERY OF FAITH

MEDITATION

→ **Spiritual quotation:** Read and reread the quotation deliberately and meditatively.

→ **Scene or Event:** Attempt to place yourself into the scene as a participant or as an observer.

→ **Mystery of Faith:** Make comparisons and analogies ("the Kingdom of Heaven is like ...").

Observe *What main ideas or impressions stood out during meditation?*

Reflect *What seems significant about these observations for your life right now?*

Converse *How is God speaking to your heart through this meditation?*

Act *What practical step can you take to bring your meditation to life in your actions today?*

JOURNAL ENTRY

"Without prayer, the soul suffocates. The deeper our prayer, the closer we come to Christ."

ST. JOHN OF THE CROSS

EVENING EXAMEN

Examine your conscience about the thoughts, words, deeds, and omissions of this day. Then, with true repentance, pray an **Act of Contrition**: "O my God, I am heartily sorry for having offended Thee, and I detest all my sins because of Thy just punishments, but most of all because they offend Thee, my God, who art all good and deserving of all my love. I firmly resolve with the help of Thy grace to sin no more and to avoid the near occasion of sin. Amen."

Our Father. Hail Mary. Glory Be.

GOD'S PRESENCE

"The angel of the Lord encamps around those who fear him, and delivers them." – **Psalm 34:7**

Subject *Write or describe the* ***quotation, scene or event,*** *or* ***mystery*** *that you will meditate on.*

○ SPIRITUAL QUOTATION | ○ SCENE OR EVENT | ○ MYSTERY OF FAITH

MEDITATION

→ **Spiritual quotation:** Read and reread the quotation deliberately and meditatively.

→ **Scene or Event:** Attempt to place yourself into the scene as a participant or as an observer.

→ **Mystery of Faith:** Make comparisons and analogies ("the Kingdom of Heaven is like ...").

Observe *What main ideas or impressions stood out during meditation?*

Reflect *What seems significant about these observations for your life right now?*

Converse *How is God speaking to your heart through this meditation?*

Act *What practical step can you take to bring your meditation to life in your actions today?*

JOURNAL ENTRY

"We must pray without tiring, for the salvation of mankind does not depend upon material success ... but on Jesus alone."

ST. FRANCES XAVIER CABRINI

EVENING EXAMEN

Examine your conscience about the thoughts, words, deeds, and omissions of this day. Then, with true repentance, pray an **Act of Contrition**: "O my God, I am heartily sorry for having offended Thee, and I detest all my sins because of Thy just punishments, but most of all because they offend Thee, my God, who art all good and deserving of all my love. I firmly resolve with the help of Thy grace to sin no more and to avoid the near occasion of sin. Amen."

Our Father. Hail Mary. Glory Be.

GOD'S PRESENCE

"For the Lord will be your confidence and will keep your foot from being caught." – **Proverbs 3:26**

Subject *Write or describe the **quotation, scene or event,** or **mystery** that you will meditate on.*

○ SPIRITUAL QUOTATION | ○ SCENE OR EVENT | ○ MYSTERY OF FAITH

MEDITATION

→ **Spiritual quotation:** Read and reread the quotation deliberately and meditatively.

→ **Scene or Event:** Attempt to place yourself into the scene as a participant or as an observer.

→ **Mystery of Faith:** Make comparisons and analogies ("the Kingdom of Heaven is like ...").

Observe *What main ideas or impressions stood out during meditation?*

Reflect *What seems significant about these observations for your life right now?*

Converse *How is God speaking to your heart through this meditation?*

Act *What practical step can you take to bring your meditation to life in your actions today?*

JOURNAL ENTRY

"Prayer is the oxygen of the soul, without which it cannot live the life of grace."

ST. PIO OF PIETRELCINA (PADRE PIO)

EVENING EXAMEN

Examine your conscience about the thoughts, words, deeds, and omissions of this day. Then, with true repentance, pray an **Act of Contrition**: "O my God, I am heartily sorry for having offended Thee, and I detest all my sins because of Thy just punishments, but most of all because they offend Thee, my God, who art all good and deserving of all my love. I firmly resolve with the help of Thy grace to sin no more and to avoid the near occasion of sin. Amen."

Our Father. Hail Mary. Glory Be.

Session 75 | / / | Source: | Adoration? Y / N

GOD'S PRESENCE

"The Lord is my portion; I promise to keep your words." – **Psalm 119:57**

Subject *Write or describe the **quotation, scene or event,** or **mystery** that you will meditate on.*

○ SPIRITUAL QUOTATION | ○ SCENE OR EVENT | ○ MYSTERY OF FAITH

MEDITATION

→ **Spiritual quotation:** Read and reread the quotation deliberately and meditatively.

→ **Scene or Event:** Attempt to place yourself into the scene as a participant or as an observer.

→ **Mystery of Faith:** Make comparisons and analogies ("the Kingdom of Heaven is like ...").

Observe *What main ideas or impressions stood out during meditation?*

Reflect *What seems significant about these observations for your life right now?*

Converse *How is God speaking to your heart through this meditation?*

Act *What practical step can you take to bring your meditation to life in your actions today?*

JOURNAL ENTRY

"Listen to the voice of God in silence. Even a single moment of true prayer can change your whole day."

ST. JOHN PAUL II

EVENING EXAMEN

Examine your conscience about the thoughts, words, deeds, and omissions of this day. Then, with true repentance, pray an **Act of Contrition**: "O my God, I am heartily sorry for having offended Thee, and I detest all my sins because of Thy just punishments, but most of all because they offend Thee, my God, who art all good and deserving of all my love. I firmly resolve with the help of Thy grace to sin no more and to avoid the near occasion of sin. Amen."

Our Father. Hail Mary. Glory Be.

Session 76 | / / | Source: | Adoration? Y / N

GOD'S PRESENCE

"God is gracious and merciful, and will not turn away his face from you, if you return to him." – **2 Chronicles 30:9**

Subject *Write or describe the* ***quotation, scene or event,*** *or* ***mystery*** *that you will meditate on.*

○ SPIRITUAL QUOTATION | ○ SCENE OR EVENT | ○ MYSTERY OF FAITH

MEDITATION

→ **Spiritual quotation:** Read and reread the quotation deliberately and meditatively.

→ **Scene or Event:** Attempt to place yourself into the scene as a participant or as an observer.

→ **Mystery of Faith:** Make comparisons and analogies ("the Kingdom of Heaven is like ...").

Observe *What main ideas or impressions stood out during meditation?*

Reflect *What seems significant about these observations for your life right now?*

Converse *How is God speaking to your heart through this meditation?*

Act *What practical step can you take to bring your meditation to life in your actions today?*

JOURNAL ENTRY

"God does not delay to hear our prayers, because He already grants more than we ask."

ST. AUGUSTINE OF HIPPO

EVENING EXAMEN

Examine your conscience about the thoughts, words, deeds, and omissions of this day. Then, with true repentance, pray an **Act of Contrition**: "O my God, I am heartily sorry for having offended Thee, and I detest all my sins because of Thy just punishments, but most of all because they offend Thee, my God, who art all good and deserving of all my love. I firmly resolve with the help of Thy grace to sin no more and to avoid the near occasion of sin. Amen."

Our Father. Hail Mary. Glory Be.

Session 77 | / / | Source: | Adoration? Y / N

GOD'S PRESENCE

"Do not fear, you worm Jacob ... I will help you, says the Lord; your Redeemer is the Holy One of Israel." – **Isaiah 41:14**

Subject *Write or describe the* ***quotation, scene or event,*** *or* ***mystery*** *that you will meditate on.*

○ SPIRITUAL QUOTATION | ○ SCENE OR EVENT | ○ MYSTERY OF FAITH

MEDITATION

→ **Spiritual quotation:** Read and reread the quotation deliberately and meditatively.

→ **Scene or Event:** Attempt to place yourself into the scene as a participant or as an observer.

→ **Mystery of Faith:** Make comparisons and analogies ("the Kingdom of Heaven is like ...").

Observe *What main ideas or impressions stood out during meditation?*

Reflect *What seems significant about these observations for your life right now?*

Converse *How is God speaking to your heart through this meditation?*

Act *What practical step can you take to bring your meditation to life in your actions today?*

JOURNAL ENTRY

"We must empty purgatory with our prayers."

ST. PIO OF PIETRELCINA (PADRE PIO)

EVENING EXAMEN

Examine your conscience about the thoughts, words, deeds, and omissions of this day. Then, with true repentance, pray an **Act of Contrition**: "O my God, I am heartily sorry for having offended Thee, and I detest all my sins because of Thy just punishments, but most of all because they offend Thee, my God, who art all good and deserving of all my love. I firmly resolve with the help of Thy grace to sin no more and to avoid the near occasion of sin. Amen."

Our Father. Hail Mary. Glory Be.

Session 78 | / / | Source: | Adoration? Y / N

GOD'S PRESENCE

"... Those who wait for the Lord shall renew their strength, they shall mount up with wings like eagles ..." – **Isaiah 40:31**

Subject *Write or describe the* ***quotation, scene or event,*** *or* ***mystery*** *that you will meditate on.*

○ SPIRITUAL QUOTATION | ○ SCENE OR EVENT | ○ MYSTERY OF FAITH

MEDITATION

→ **Spiritual quotation:** Read and reread the quotation deliberately and meditatively.

→ **Scene or Event:** Attempt to place yourself into the scene as a participant or as an observer.

→ **Mystery of Faith:** Make comparisons and analogies ("the Kingdom of Heaven is like ...").

Observe *What main ideas or impressions stood out during meditation?*

Reflect *What seems significant about these observations for your life right now?*

Converse *How is God speaking to your heart through this meditation?*

Act *What practical step can you take to bring your meditation to life in your actions today?*

JOURNAL ENTRY

"Prayer is the best armor we have. It is the key which opens the heart of God."

ST. PIO OF PIETRELCINA (PADRE PIO)

EVENING EXAMEN

Examine your conscience about the thoughts, words, deeds, and omissions of this day. Then, with true repentance, pray an **Act of Contrition**: "O my God, I am heartily sorry for having offended Thee, and I detest all my sins because of Thy just punishments, but most of all because they offend Thee, my God, who art all good and deserving of all my love. I firmly resolve with the help of Thy grace to sin no more and to avoid the near occasion of sin. Amen."

Our Father. Hail Mary. Glory Be.

Session 79 | / / | Source: | Adoration? Y / N

GOD'S PRESENCE

"I will live in them and walk among them, and I will be their God, and they shall be my people." **– 2 Corinthians 6:16**

Subject *Write or describe the **quotation, scene or event,** or **mystery** that you will meditate on.*

○ SPIRITUAL QUOTATION | ○ SCENE OR EVENT | ○ MYSTERY OF FAITH

MEDITATION

→ **Spiritual quotation:** Read and reread the quotation deliberately and meditatively.

→ **Scene or Event:** Attempt to place yourself into the scene as a participant or as an observer.

→ **Mystery of Faith:** Make comparisons and analogies ("the Kingdom of Heaven is like ...").

Observe *What main ideas or impressions stood out during meditation?*

Reflect *What seems significant about these observations for your life right now?*

Converse *How is God speaking to your heart through this meditation?*

Act *What practical step can you take to bring your meditation to life in your actions today?*

JOURNAL ENTRY

"Prayer unites us with the One we seek and makes us worthy of His love."

ST. GREGORY OF NYSSA

EVENING EXAMEN

Examine your conscience about the thoughts, words, deeds, and omissions of this day. Then, with true repentance, pray an **Act of Contrition**: "O my God, I am heartily sorry for having offended Thee, and I detest all my sins because of Thy just punishments, but most of all because they offend Thee, my God, who art all good and deserving of all my love. I firmly resolve with the help of Thy grace to sin no more and to avoid the near occasion of sin. Amen."

Our Father. Hail Mary. Glory Be.

Session 80 | / / | Source: | Adoration? Y / N

GOD'S PRESENCE

"I keep the Lord always before me; because he is at my right hand, I shall not be moved." – **Psalm 16:8**

Subject *Write or describe the **quotation, scene or event,** or **mystery** that you will meditate on.*

○ SPIRITUAL QUOTATION | ○ SCENE OR EVENT | ○ MYSTERY OF FAITH

MEDITATION

→ **Spiritual quotation:** Read and reread the quotation deliberately and meditatively.

→ **Scene or Event:** Attempt to place yourself into the scene as a participant or as an observer.

→ **Mystery of Faith:** Make comparisons and analogies ("the Kingdom of Heaven is like ...").

Observe *What main ideas or impressions stood out during meditation?*

Reflect *What seems significant about these observations for your life right now?*

Converse *How is God speaking to your heart through this meditation?*

Act *What practical step can you take to bring your meditation to life in your actions today?*

JOURNAL ENTRY

"Let prayer delight thee more than any of the fine dishes of the world."

ST. CHARLES BORROMEO

EVENING EXAMEN

Examine your conscience about the thoughts, words, deeds, and omissions of this day. Then, with true repentance, pray an **Act of Contrition**: "O my God, I am heartily sorry for having offended Thee, and I detest all my sins because of Thy just punishments, but most of all because they offend Thee, my God, who art all good and deserving of all my love. I firmly resolve with the help of Thy grace to sin no more and to avoid the near occasion of sin. Amen."

Our Father. Hail Mary. Glory Be.

Session 81 | / / | Source: | Adoration? Y / N

GOD'S PRESENCE

"By this we know that we abide in him and he in us, because he has given us of his Spirit." – **1 John 4:13**

Subject *Write or describe the **quotation, scene or event,** or **mystery** that you will meditate on.*

○ SPIRITUAL QUOTATION | ○ SCENE OR EVENT | ○ MYSTERY OF FAITH

MEDITATION

→ **Spiritual quotation:** Read and reread the quotation deliberately and meditatively.

→ **Scene or Event:** Attempt to place yourself into the scene as a participant or as an observer.

→ **Mystery of Faith:** Make comparisons and analogies ("the Kingdom of Heaven is like ...").

Observe *What main ideas or impressions stood out during meditation?*

Reflect *What seems significant about these observations for your life right now?*

Converse *How is God speaking to your heart through this meditation?*

Act *What practical step can you take to bring your meditation to life in your actions today?*

JOURNAL ENTRY

"Prayer purifies us, reading instructs us. Both are good when both are possible. Otherwise, prayer is better than reading."

ST. ISIDORE OF SEVILLE

EVENING EXAMEN

Examine your conscience about the thoughts, words, deeds, and omissions of this day. Then, with true repentance, pray an **Act of Contrition**: "O my God, I am heartily sorry for having offended Thee, and I detest all my sins because of Thy just punishments, but most of all because they offend Thee, my God, who art all good and deserving of all my love. I firmly resolve with the help of Thy grace to sin no more and to avoid the near occasion of sin. Amen."

Our Father. Hail Mary. Glory Be.

Session 82 | / / | Source: | Adoration? Y / N

GOD'S PRESENCE

"Am I a God near by, says the Lord, and not a God far off?" – **Jeremiah 23:23**

Subject *Write or describe the* ***quotation, scene or event,*** *or* ***mystery*** *that you will meditate on.*

○ SPIRITUAL QUOTATION | ○ SCENE OR EVENT | ○ MYSTERY OF FAITH

MEDITATION

→ **Spiritual quotation:** Read and reread the quotation deliberately and meditatively.

→ **Scene or Event:** Attempt to place yourself into the scene as a participant or as an observer.

→ **Mystery of Faith:** Make comparisons and analogies ("the Kingdom of Heaven is like ...").

Observe *What main ideas or impressions stood out during meditation?*

Reflect *What seems significant about these observations for your life right now?*

Converse *How is God speaking to your heart through this meditation?*

Act *What practical step can you take to bring your meditation to life in your actions today?*

JOURNAL ENTRY

"When we pray, the voice of the heart must be heard more than that proceeding from the mouth."

ST. BONAVENTURE

EVENING EXAMEN

Examine your conscience about the thoughts, words, deeds, and omissions of this day. Then, with true repentance, pray an **Act of Contrition**: "O my God, I am heartily sorry for having offended Thee, and I detest all my sins because of Thy just punishments, but most of all because they offend Thee, my God, who art all good and deserving of all my love. I firmly resolve with the help of Thy grace to sin no more and to avoid the near occasion of sin. Amen."

Our Father. Hail Mary. Glory Be.

Session 83 | / / | Source: | Adoration? Y / N

GOD'S PRESENCE

"Surely the righteous shall give thanks to your name; the upright shall live in your presence." – **Psalm 140:13**

Subject *Write or describe the* ***quotation, scene or event,*** *or* ***mystery*** *that you will meditate on.*

○ SPIRITUAL QUOTATION | ○ SCENE OR EVENT | ○ MYSTERY OF FAITH

MEDITATION

→ **Spiritual quotation:** Read and reread the quotation deliberately and meditatively.

→ **Scene or Event:** Attempt to place yourself into the scene as a participant or as an observer.

→ **Mystery of Faith:** Make comparisons and analogies ("the Kingdom of Heaven is like ...").

Observe *What main ideas or impressions stood out during meditation?*

Reflect *What seems significant about these observations for your life right now?*

Converse *How is God speaking to your heart through this meditation?*

Act *What practical step can you take to bring your meditation to life in your actions today?*

JOURNAL ENTRY

"Let nothing trouble you, let nothing frighten you. Everything passes away except God."

ST. TERESA OF ÁVILA

EVENING EXAMEN

Examine your conscience about the thoughts, words, deeds, and omissions of this day. Then, with true repentance, pray an **Act of Contrition**: "O my God, I am heartily sorry for having offended Thee, and I detest all my sins because of Thy just punishments, but most of all because they offend Thee, my God, who art all good and deserving of all my love. I firmly resolve with the help of Thy grace to sin no more and to avoid the near occasion of sin. Amen."

Our Father. Hail Mary. Glory Be.

Session 84 | / / | Source: | Adoration? Y / N

GOD'S PRESENCE

"Thus says the Lord, your Redeemer: ... I am the Lord your God, who teaches you for your own good ..." – **Isaiah 48:17**

Subject *Write or describe the* ***quotation, scene or event,*** *or* ***mystery*** *that you will meditate on.*

○ SPIRITUAL QUOTATION | ○ SCENE OR EVENT | ○ MYSTERY OF FAITH

MEDITATION

→ **Spiritual quotation:** Read and reread the quotation deliberately and meditatively.

→ **Scene or Event:** Attempt to place yourself into the scene as a participant or as an observer.

→ **Mystery of Faith:** Make comparisons and analogies ("the Kingdom of Heaven is like ...").

Observe *What main ideas or impressions stood out during meditation?*

Reflect *What seems significant about these observations for your life right now?*

Converse *How is God speaking to your heart through this meditation?*

Act *What practical step can you take to bring your meditation to life in your actions today?*

JOURNAL ENTRY

"God gives Himself to the soul when the soul seeks Him through prayer."

ST. TERESA BENEDICTA OF THE CROSS (EDITH STEIN)

EVENING EXAMEN

Examine your conscience about the thoughts, words, deeds, and omissions of this day. Then, with true repentance, pray an **Act of Contrition**: "O my God, I am heartily sorry for having offended Thee, and I detest all my sins because of Thy just punishments, but most of all because they offend Thee, my God, who art all good and deserving of all my love. I firmly resolve with the help of Thy grace to sin no more and to avoid the near occasion of sin. Amen."

Our Father. Hail Mary. Glory Be.

Session 85 | / / | Source: | Adoration? Y / N

GOD'S PRESENCE

"Do not let your hearts be troubled. Believe in God, believe also in me." – **John 14:1**

Subject *Write or describe the* ***quotation, scene or event,*** *or* ***mystery*** *that you will meditate on.*

○ SPIRITUAL QUOTATION | ○ SCENE OR EVENT | ○ MYSTERY OF FAITH

MEDITATION

→ **Spiritual quotation:** Read and reread the quotation deliberately and meditatively.

→ **Scene or Event:** Attempt to place yourself into the scene as a participant or as an observer.

→ **Mystery of Faith:** Make comparisons and analogies ("the Kingdom of Heaven is like ...").

Observe *What main ideas or impressions stood out during meditation?*

Reflect *What seems significant about these observations for your life right now?*

Converse *How is God speaking to your heart through this meditation?*

Act *What practical step can you take to bring your meditation to life in your actions today?*

JOURNAL ENTRY

"The fruit of prayer is peace. The fruit of prayer is love. The fruit of love is service."

ST. TERESA OF CALCUTTA

EVENING EXAMEN

Examine your conscience about the thoughts, words, deeds, and omissions of this day. Then, with true repentance, pray an **Act of Contrition**: "O my God, I am heartily sorry for having offended Thee, and I detest all my sins because of Thy just punishments, but most of all because they offend Thee, my God, who art all good and deserving of all my love. I firmly resolve with the help of Thy grace to sin no more and to avoid the near occasion of sin. Amen."

Our Father. Hail Mary. Glory Be.

Session 86 | / / | Source: | Adoration? Y / N

GOD'S PRESENCE

"For God did not give us a spirit of cowardice, but rather a spirit of power and of love and of self-discipline." – **2 Timothy 1:7**

Subject *Write or describe the **quotation, scene or event,** or **mystery** that you will meditate on.*

○ SPIRITUAL QUOTATION | ○ SCENE OR EVENT | ○ MYSTERY OF FAITH

MEDITATION

→ **Spiritual quotation:** Read and reread the quotation deliberately and meditatively.

→ **Scene or Event:** Attempt to place yourself into the scene as a participant or as an observer.

→ **Mystery of Faith:** Make comparisons and analogies ("the Kingdom of Heaven is like ...").

Observe *What main ideas or impressions stood out during meditation?*

Reflect *What seems significant about these observations for your life right now?*

Converse *How is God speaking to your heart through this meditation?*

Act *What practical step can you take to bring your meditation to life in your actions today?*

JOURNAL ENTRY

"In the evening, when you go to sleep, reflect on the day: ask for forgiveness for your faults, give thanks for blessings, and pray for tomorrow."

ST. JOHN BOSCO

EVENING EXAMEN

Examine your conscience about the thoughts, words, deeds, and omissions of this day. Then, with true repentance, pray an **Act of Contrition**: "O my God, I am heartily sorry for having offended Thee, and I detest all my sins because of Thy just punishments, but most of all because they offend Thee, my God, who art all good and deserving of all my love. I firmly resolve with the help of Thy grace to sin no more and to avoid the near occasion of sin. Amen."

Our Father. Hail Mary. Glory Be.

Session 87 | / / | Source: | Adoration? Y / N

GOD'S PRESENCE

"Cast all your anxiety on him, because he cares for you." – **1 Peter 5:7**

Subject *Write or describe the **quotation, scene or event,** or **mystery** that you will meditate on.*

○ SPIRITUAL QUOTATION | ○ SCENE OR EVENT | ○ MYSTERY OF FAITH

MEDITATION

→ **Spiritual quotation:** Read and reread the quotation deliberately and meditatively.

→ **Scene or Event:** Attempt to place yourself into the scene as a participant or as an observer.

→ **Mystery of Faith:** Make comparisons and analogies ("the Kingdom of Heaven is like ...").

Observe *What main ideas or impressions stood out during meditation?*

Reflect *What seems significant about these observations for your life right now?*

Converse *How is God speaking to your heart through this meditation?*

Act *What practical step can you take to bring your meditation to life in your actions today?*

JOURNAL ENTRY

"When you pray, you open your heart to God. Prayer is the key to opening the doors of Heaven."

ST. JOHN CHRYSOSTOM

EVENING EXAMEN

Examine your conscience about the thoughts, words, deeds, and omissions of this day. Then, with true repentance, pray an **Act of Contrition**: "O my God, I am heartily sorry for having offended Thee, and I detest all my sins because of Thy just punishments, but most of all because they offend Thee, my God, who art all good and deserving of all my love. I firmly resolve with the help of Thy grace to sin no more and to avoid the near occasion of sin. Amen."

Our Father. Hail Mary. Glory Be.

Session 88 | / / | Source: | Adoration? Y / N

GOD'S PRESENCE

"You have made known to me the ways of life; you will make me full of gladness with your presence." – **Acts 2:28**

Subject *Write or describe the* ***quotation, scene or event,*** *or* ***mystery*** *that you will meditate on.*

○ SPIRITUAL QUOTATION | ○ SCENE OR EVENT | ○ MYSTERY OF FAITH

MEDITATION

→ **Spiritual quotation:** Read and reread the quotation deliberately and meditatively.

→ **Scene or Event:** Attempt to place yourself into the scene as a participant or as an observer.

→ **Mystery of Faith:** Make comparisons and analogies ("the Kingdom of Heaven is like ...").

Observe *What main ideas or impressions stood out during meditation?*

Reflect *What seems significant about these observations for your life right now?*

Converse *How is God speaking to your heart through this meditation?*

Act *What practical step can you take to bring your meditation to life in your actions today?*

JOURNAL ENTRY

"Ask and you will receive, seek and you will find; knock and the door will be opened to you."

MATTHEW 7:7

EVENING EXAMEN

Examine your conscience about the thoughts, words, deeds, and omissions of this day. Then, with true repentance, pray an **Act of Contrition**: "O my God, I am heartily sorry for having offended Thee, and I detest all my sins because of Thy just punishments, but most of all because they offend Thee, my God, who art all good and deserving of all my love. I firmly resolve with the help of Thy grace to sin no more and to avoid the near occasion of sin. Amen."

Our Father. Hail Mary. Glory Be.

Session 89 | / / | Source: | Adoration? Y / N

GOD'S PRESENCE

"Commit your way to the Lord; trust in him, and he will act." – **Psalm 37:5**

Subject *Write or describe the* ***quotation, scene or event,*** *or* ***mystery*** *that you will meditate on.*

○ SPIRITUAL QUOTATION | ○ SCENE OR EVENT | ○ MYSTERY OF FAITH

MEDITATION

→ **Spiritual quotation:** Read and reread the quotation deliberately and meditatively.

→ **Scene or Event:** Attempt to place yourself into the scene as a participant or as an observer.

→ **Mystery of Faith:** Make comparisons and analogies ("the Kingdom of Heaven is like ...").

Observe *What main ideas or impressions stood out during meditation?*

Reflect *What seems significant about these observations for your life right now?*

Converse *How is God speaking to your heart through this meditation?*

Act *What practical step can you take to bring your meditation to life in your actions today?*

JOURNAL ENTRY

"Nothing is more powerful than prayer. It turns the heart of stone into a heart of flesh."

ST. AUGUSTINE OF HIPPO

EVENING EXAMEN

Examine your conscience about the thoughts, words, deeds, and omissions of this day. Then, with true repentance, pray an **Act of Contrition**: "O my God, I am heartily sorry for having offended Thee, and I detest all my sins because of Thy just punishments, but most of all because they offend Thee, my God, who art all good and deserving of all my love. I firmly resolve with the help of Thy grace to sin no more and to avoid the near occasion of sin. Amen."

Our Father. Hail Mary. Glory Be.

Session 90 | / / | Source: | Adoration? Y / N

GOD'S PRESENCE

"For the Lord your God is a merciful God; he will neither abandon you nor destroy you ..." – **Deuteronomy 4:31**

Subject *Write or describe the **quotation, scene or event,** or **mystery** that you will meditate on.*

○ SPIRITUAL QUOTATION | ○ SCENE OR EVENT | ○ MYSTERY OF FAITH

MEDITATION

→ **Spiritual quotation:** Read and reread the quotation deliberately and meditatively.

→ **Scene or Event:** Attempt to place yourself into the scene as a participant or as an observer.

→ **Mystery of Faith:** Make comparisons and analogies ("the Kingdom of Heaven is like ...").

Observe *What main ideas or impressions stood out during meditation?*

Reflect *What seems significant about these observations for your life right now?*

Converse *How is God speaking to your heart through this meditation?*

Act *What practical step can you take to bring your meditation to life in your actions today?*

JOURNAL ENTRY

"Begin all your prayers with an act of humility, so that God may give you the grace to pray well."

ST. VINCENT DE PAUL

EVENING EXAMEN

Examine your conscience about the thoughts, words, deeds, and omissions of this day. Then, with true repentance, pray an **Act of Contrition**: "O my God, I am heartily sorry for having offended Thee, and I detest all my sins because of Thy just punishments, but most of all because they offend Thee, my God, who art all good and deserving of all my love. I firmly resolve with the help of Thy grace to sin no more and to avoid the near occasion of sin. Amen."

Our Father. Hail Mary. Glory Be.

FINAL REFLECTION

A NEW BEGINNING IN PRAYER

As you complete this three-month journey of meditation, take a moment to reflect on the deeper transformation that has taken place. Prayer is the foundation of our relationship with God, and while this journal has come to an end, the journey of growing in love, wisdom, and holiness continues. Reflect deeply on what God has done in your heart and how you will carry this into your life moving forward.

How has your relationship with God changed through these three months of meditation practice, and what specific steps will you take to continue deepening your prayer life in the coming months?

STREAK TRACKER

START DATE	1	2	3	4	5	6	7	8	9	10	11	12	13
6/20/2025	✓	✓	✓	✓	✓	✓	✓	✓	✓	✓	✓	✓	✗
7/4/2025	✓	✓	✓	✓	✓	✓	✓	✓	✓	✓	✓	✓	✓
	☐	☐	☐	☐	☐	☐	☐	☐	☐	☐	☐	☐	☐
	☐	☐	☐	☐	☐	☐	☐	☐	☐	☐	☐	☐	☐
	☐	☐	☐	☐	☐	☐	☐	☐	☐	☐	☐	☐	☐
	☐	☐	☐	☐	☐	☐	☐	☐	☐	☐	☐	☐	☐
	☐	☐	☐	☐	☐	☐	☐	☐	☐	☐	☐	☐	☐
	☐	☐	☐	☐	☐	☐	☐	☐	☐	☐	☐	☐	☐
	☐	☐	☐	☐	☐	☐	☐	☐	☐	☐	☐	☐	☐
	☐	☐	☐	☐	☐	☐	☐	☐	☐	☐	☐	☐	☐
	☐	☐	☐	☐	☐	☐	☐	☐	☐	☐	☐	☐	☐
	☐	☐	☐	☐	☐	☐	☐	☐	☐	☐	☐	☐	☐
	☐	☐	☐	☐	☐	☐	☐	☐	☐	☐	☐	☐	☐
	☐	☐	☐	☐	☐	☐	☐	☐	☐	☐	☐	☐	☐
	☐	☐	☐	☐	☐	☐	☐	☐	☐	☐	☐	☐	☐
	☐	☐	☐	☐	☐	☐	☐	☐	☐	☐	☐	☐	☐
	☐	☐	☐	☐	☐	☐	☐	☐	☐	☐	☐	☐	☐
	☐	☐	☐	☐	☐	☐	☐	☐	☐	☐	☐	☐	☐
	☐	☐	☐	☐	☐	☐	☐	☐	☐	☐	☐	☐	☐
	☐	☐	☐	☐	☐	☐	☐	☐	☐	☐	☐	☐	☐
	☐	☐	☐	☐	☐	☐	☐	☐	☐	☐	☐	☐	☐
	☐	☐	☐	☐	☐	☐	☐	☐	☐	☐	☐	☐	☐
	☐	☐	☐	☐	☐	☐	☐	☐	☐	☐	☐	☐	☐
	☐	☐	☐	☐	☐	☐	☐	☐	☐	☐	☐	☐	☐
	☐	☐	☐	☐	☐	☐	☐	☐	☐	☐	☐	☐	☐
	☐	☐	☐	☐	☐	☐	☐	☐	☐	☐	☐	☐	☐
	☐	☐	☐	☐	☐	☐	☐	☐	☐	☐	☐	☐	☐

Use the Streak Tracker to help you succeed. Write the start date of your streak in the "Start Date" column. When you break your streak, mark "x" and start a new row. The first two rows are an example—keep trying until you get a full 31-day streak!

14	15	16	17	18	19	20	21	22	23	24	25	26	27	28	29	30	31
☐	☐	☐	☐	☐	☐	☐	☐	☐	☐	☐	☐	☐	☐	☐	☐	☐	☐
☑	☑	☑	☑	☑	☐	☐	☐	☐	☐	☐	☐	☐	☐	☐	☐	☐	☐
☐	☐	☐	☐	☐	☐	☐	☐	☐	☐	☐	☐	☐	☐	☐	☐	☐	☐
☐	☐	☐	☐	☐	☐	☐	☐	☐	☐	☐	☐	☐	☐	☐	☐	☐	☐
☐	☐	☐	☐	☐	☐	☐	☐	☐	☐	☐	☐	☐	☐	☐	☐	☐	☐
☐	☐	☐	☐	☐	☐	☐	☐	☐	☐	☐	☐	☐	☐	☐	☐	☐	☐
☐	☐	☐	☐	☐	☐	☐	☐	☐	☐	☐	☐	☐	☐	☐	☐	☐	☐
☐	☐	☐	☐	☐	☐	☐	☐	☐	☐	☐	☐	☐	☐	☐	☐	☐	☐
☐	☐	☐	☐	☐	☐	☐	☐	☐	☐	☐	☐	☐	☐	☐	☐	☐	☐
☐	☐	☐	☐	☐	☐	☐	☐	☐	☐	☐	☐	☐	☐	☐	☐	☐	☐
☐	☐	☐	☐	☐	☐	☐	☐	☐	☐	☐	☐	☐	☐	☐	☐	☐	☐
☐	☐	☐	☐	☐	☐	☐	☐	☐	☐	☐	☐	☐	☐	☐	☐	☐	☐
☐	☐	☐	☐	☐	☐	☐	☐	☐	☐	☐	☐	☐	☐	☐	☐	☐	☐
☐	☐	☐	☐	☐	☐	☐	☐	☐	☐	☐	☐	☐	☐	☐	☐	☐	☐
☐	☐	☐	☐	☐	☐	☐	☐	☐	☐	☐	☐	☐	☐	☐	☐	☐	☐
☐	☐	☐	☐	☐	☐	☐	☐	☐	☐	☐	☐	☐	☐	☐	☐	☐	☐
☐	☐	☐	☐	☐	☐	☐	☐	☐	☐	☐	☐	☐	☐	☐	☐	☐	☐
☐	☐	☐	☐	☐	☐	☐	☐	☐	☐	☐	☐	☐	☐	☐	☐	☐	☐
☐	☐	☐	☐	☐	☐	☐	☐	☐	☐	☐	☐	☐	☐	☐	☐	☐	☐
☐	☐	☐	☐	☐	☐	☐	☐	☐	☐	☐	☐	☐	☐	☐	☐	☐	☐
☐	☐	☐	☐	☐	☐	☐	☐	☐	☐	☐	☐	☐	☐	☐	☐	☐	☐
☐	☐	☐	☐	☐	☐	☐	☐	☐	☐	☐	☐	☐	☐	☐	☐	☐	☐
☐	☐	☐	☐	☐	☐	☐	☐	☐	☐	☐	☐	☐	☐	☐	☐	☐	☐
☐	☐	☐	☐	☐	☐	☐	☐	☐	☐	☐	☐	☐	☐	☐	☐	☐	☐
☐	☐	☐	☐	☐	☐	☐	☐	☐	☐	☐	☐	☐	☐	☐	☐	☐	☐
☐	☐	☐	☐	☐	☐	☐	☐	☐	☐	☐	☐	☐	☐	☐	☐	☐	☐
☐	☐	☐	☐	☐	☐	☐	☐	☐	☐	☐	☐	☐	☐	☐	☐	☐	☐

MORE SAINTMAKER PRODUCTS

THE SAINTMAKER CATHOLIC LIFE PLANNER

The original Saintmaker product, The Saintmaker is a one-of-a-kind guided spiritual journal and life planning system to help you create the life you dream of, become a more fulfilled person, and deepen your faith.

HOLY HABITS JOURNAL

Ready to elevate your spiritual practice? The Saintmaker Holy Habits Journal offers you an inspiring 60-day adventure, combining practical steps with contemplative depth to transform your faith and enrich your spiritual life.

DAILYSAINT 5-MINUTE SPIRITUAL JOURNAL

Powered by modern positive psychology and the ancient traditions of Christian mystics, DailySaint will bookend your day with a prayerful morning and evening routine to help you consistently see God's hand in your life.

SHARE

@saintmakerthe #pilgrimofprayer

SHOP

www.thesaintmaker.com

Pilgrim of Prayer Journal
Version 1.0

Imprint: Saintmaker / Author: Saintmaker

ISBN: 979-8-88911-486-4

Published by Sophia Institute Press, 18 Celina Ave (Unit 1), Nashua, NH 03063

Designed in the United States / Printed in China